It Started with the Apple

The Role of Food in the Faith Journey

By Carolyn Clayton

PUBLISH AMERICA

PublishAmerica
Baltimore

First printing

PublishAmerica has allowed this work to remain exactly as the author intended, verbatim, without editorial input.

ISBN: 1-60813-618-3
PUBLISHED BY PUBLISHAMERICA, LLLP
www.publishamerica.com
Baltimore

Printed in the United States of America

It Started with the Apple

*The Role of Food
in the Faith Journey*

Introduction

It started with the apple, didn't it—the striking use of something to eat as an access code to the human soul? It continues today in church fellowship halls across America.

In the Garden of Eden Satan tempted Adam and Eve with the forbidden fruit because he knew that everything else was already lavished upon them. Offering them Paradise wasn't going to work because they already had it. So he offered a luscious, tempting edible. "Why not taste this, what's the harm, it was put here for you ." Of further significance is the choice of food as the temptation. It is interesting to note that he did not try to tempt them with water from a forbidden pool, or a fragrant blossom, or a beautiful stone. Quite often we have heard that the way to a man's heart is through his stomach; I would like to suggest to you that a route to man's soul can begin similarly.

What can be learned from eating with Abraham? Or the disciples? Or your next door neighbor? How did eating together change when Jesus walked the earth? There are lots of stories in the Bible about this, some of which will be highlighted in my book.

As history moved on, the Middle Ages saw the introduction of lemons, oranges, artichokes, beans, and asparagus for the wealthy, most of these things coming via the new trade routes to the Orient. Columbus' discovery of the New World also enabled new and exotic additions to the diet. These were added to the table along with either pork or chicken (raising beef required more land and thus only the very wealthy could afford it.). In the seventeenth and eighteenth centuries dinners for the upper class changed from being starkly bare to being lavish. Gatherings became lush social and political events. This heralded the appearance of dining rooms and banquet halls. Meanwhile, brown bread, porridge, cabbage, and beets remained the staples of the poor. Other strong influences in these early times were famines and the scarcity of foodstuffs.

As great strides were made in the availability of food and techniques for its preservation, meals became more diverse. Man learned that removing moisture from items greatly reduced their spoilage, and so they hung food in strong winds or exposed it to the hot sun. Vegetables, eggs, and fish were pickled. Eating was changing its posture from one of survival to one of enjoyment.

If secular eating was changing, so was the Christian table. The Bible gives us stories about food whether symbolic or real, that connect man to temptation and to life. We will also see that food and fellowship come to be a positive force as the Christian religion develops, and we will examine some events that illustrate this. When considered, it is startling to see how an insignificant activity like eating became significant. Initially, the setting in which people ate was inconsequential, because eating was to live, not an occasion.

During the years before the birth of Christ there was no separate room for dining as there was no special need to sit at length over a meal. Rudimentary sawhorses with boards and cloths thrown over them enabled a meal regardless of location.

We will journey from sawhorse tables into modern America's church fellowship halls. Although my focus in *It Started With The Apple* is current church food service in America, I thought it appropriate to start where it actually started, and thumbnail events through the centuries leading to the present. The more I investigated, the more I became convinced that the vital role played by food has been obscured. We have highlighted what happened while we ate without noticing the importance of what we ate and where we ate it. What we will be interested in here is the journey of food and eating through the Bible and the centuries into present-day America, specifically in her churches.

Probably there is no more unexplored area of the church than its kitchen. It seems distant, remote, not a real part of the church or its outreach. Many members have never set foot in there unless it was to return a dirty dish. It can seem out of sync with the mission of the church, and the employees there unapproachable. We wonder what they do if it's not Wednesday.

So, a look into this unexplored area seems appropriate. A good means of understanding church food service is to examine it from its home-style beginnings to its more-commercial setting today. To my knowledge no one has ever chronicled this journey, and admittedly biased, I will have to say that the evolution is one that begs to be shared. In researching for the book, I have actually been fascinated, amazed, by what I have learned about these churches in America. I thought I was the expert, but what I have come to realize is how much I did not know.

It Started with the Apple is my way of encouraging those who work in food service today, and informing those who do not. It is not intended to be a textbook, although there are ideas throughout the chapters. I think my book will remove some of the mystery about church food service, and take the reader on an informative and pleasant journey. I hope you will experience some of the "ah hahs" I did.

Finally, I must say that part of my education was learning that there is not a "typical" model for a church. Not anywhere. Nothing I write is intended as a blueprint for any congregation, but rather as an insight into what has worked well, and on occasion, what has not. If any of this resonates with you, or informs you, or gives you a new idea, then I will be pleased.

Diverse at their start and dissimilar in their growth, churches are each unique today. The churches I highlight in the book may or may not be like the church around the corner from you or the church you attend, but all have a rich history. My hope is that you will enjoy reading this as much as I did writing it.

Carolyn Clayton
Atlanta, Georgia
October 2008

Chapter One
The Ties That Bind—Hospitality and Food

Matthew 18:20 "For where two or three
come together in my name, there I am with them."

When we are celebrating food is nearly always a part of the picture. Welcome is a cornerstone of this, projecting the image of the church and becoming its signature. It reaches non-members of the church who will come to eat if not to be fed, and in so doing offers them an impression of what the church/religion is about. The giving of daily bread was important enough to Jesus for Him to include this when He was teaching us how to pray.

Not much has ever been written identifying food service as a ministry of the church, but it unquestionably is. Ministry is often perceived as worship, education, or music, whether consciously or not. Somewhere in the labyrinth of programs the kitchen certainly resides, but it is often not thought of as a primary part of the church. Nonetheless food service is a visual and significant ambassador of welcome and fellowship available to the congregation and the community. This is evangelism in its purest sense.

If an average meal is served with smiles and greetings it will be remembered as a wonderful experience. If an excellent meal is served with little attention to the guest, it will be remembered negatively. When the taste of the food is forgotten, it is the diner's experience that seasons his judgment about the meal. In Proverbs 15:17 we read, "Better a meal of vegetables where there is love than a fatted calf with hatred." So the quality of the food usually is secondary to the quality of welcome, and nowhere is this truer than at a church.

Food service is uniquely positioned to utilize the ministry of hospitality. Later we will talk about volunteers who give two servings of meatloaf to their friends as they pass along the food line. This is the essence of ministry, isn't it? It may not be practical, but it surely says to the guest, "You are valued here, we're glad you've come, and we know you well enough to cater to your preferences." Making guests feel at home at the church is an on-going goal, and a necessary atmosphere for growth. The "missionaries" who serve in the kitchen carry this banner proudly, having found their service niche, and those who eat pleasantly at a church leave not only with a satisfied appetite but with a replenished fondness for its work.

Hospitality means taking guests (not pointing) to the restroom or classroom where an event is being held, even if from a food production standpoint it is not practical to do so. It means clearing and cleaning buffet lines, and putting fresh napkins out, and mopping up spills cheerfully. It means assisting the elderly by carrying their plate for them, and changing menu selections to accommodate a particular request. This mission field of the church is accessed by walking just a few steps rather than journeying to a foreign land or another neighborhood. Today's churches recognize this truth, particularly do those that are growing.

It will be useful to examine foods of the Old Testament and how they were a part of daily life. Let's just revisit here that man's expulsion from the Garden of Eden was when he ate the forbidden fruit, the first food symbol in the Bible. It is interesting to observe that the Devil used an apple since food was the one need Adam and Eve had. Eating remains a basic need of people today. Here there begins an early association of food with temptation/sin, and a continuing use of food to illustrate a lesson. We will see Satan trying to tempt Jesus with food, since He was vulnerable to human needs.

The Bedouins learned to live off their animals, using their milk, or roasting a sheep or a goat. Figs and grapes were plentiful, and cheese (curds) was also part of their diet. Many of the names of places are tied directly to what was plentiful in a particular location like Beth-Phage which means "house of figs." Those who lived by the shore learned to fish and use the catch as a major part of their diet.

Under the great trees of Mamre, Abraham looked up and saw three unknown visitors (Genesis 18:1). He hurried out to meet them, bowing low to the ground. He told them to rest under a tree while he fetched water for them to wash their feet, and prepared something for them to eat. Instructing Sarah to bake some bread, he then selected a choice, tender calf and asked a servant to prepare it. He took the strangers bread, curds, milk, and the calf. Before the three "visitors" departed, they told Abraham that in one year Sarah would bear him a son. This promise became a reality. Who can say what might have happened if the strangers had been turned away? Or if they are turned away, or "turned off" today?

In Abraham's time a person's reputation was greatly identified to his hospitality, and thus even strangers were treated as highly-honored guests. Doing this was an immediate way of showing hospitality, i.e. obedience to God. In Hebrews 13:1 we are exhorted to show hospitality to strangers for by doing so "some people have entertained Angels without knowing it." The use of the word "entertain" is an interesting choice, and strongly suggests fellowship. It just isn't the same to express thoughts over the telephone or in an email as it is to share the same thoughts sitting across the table from the person and together sharing a meal. This was true in Abraham's day and it is true today also.

Some essential professions of Abraham's time were cabinetmakers, metalworkers, and jewelers. The cabinetmakers fashioned furniture and hope chests from the cedars of Lebanon often decorated with silhouettes or engraving. The metalworkers made cups and beakers, and the forms for musical instruments like the lyre. The jewelers used lapis and gold and silver to make plaques and beautiful adornments. And always there were shepherds, and those who worked in the fields, and potters, and tentmakers.

In Genesis 43:11 we learn from Jacob that his sons should take a "bakseesh" to the Grand Vizier of Egypt. He tells them to put it in their best receptacles and take it to the Vizier as a present. He recommends a little balm, a little honey, gum, laudanum, pistachio nuts, and almonds. In other words, in order to make a good impression, use your finest serving pieces and fill them with delectable foods. This is absolutely the cornerstone of church food service today.

Bread was critical to sustain life. Mostly, the patriarchs' headquarters were stationary, allowing the cultivation of grain. Abraham kept at least two kinds of flour, and Genesis tells us that Isaac and Jacob learned how to grow wheat and then grind it with a pestle on a stone mortar. Later, they would have a mill made of two circular stones that could be rotated against each other with wheat between them to produce flour. The length of time the grains were ground determined how fine the resulting flour would be.

The flour would be mixed with water and salt to make dough which was then made into flat cakes twelve to sixteen inches in diameter. This would produce unleavened bread, but soon they would learn to save out a bit of dough and put it into the next batch to produce leavened bread. Then they built a fire on a flat stone, and when it was thoroughly heated, the embers were pushed aside, and the cakes laid on. One side would be cooked, and then the process was repeated after the cake was turned over. In Hosea: 7:8 we are told that Ephraim is a flat cake, not turned over. Many people think this is where the unflattering term "half-baked" originated.

In the court of Solomon there were monthly sessions with the ministers. Their chairs arranged in semi-circles before his throne, the ministers began their reports. First would be one on the state of defenses, and then the reports of the administrative districts, and finally reports on supplies collected that would include fine flour, meal, fatted cattle, sheep, delicacies, and fowl. So food was also a major part of the economy, not just a means of sustaining life.

The details of household life in the time of Isaiah are not specifically told us, but it is likely that the food they ate was similar to that of Abraham's time with one important addition: olive oil. In the land where olive trees flourished it is reasonable to assume that the oil was extracted from the olives and used in cooking. Fruit juices were the usual beverage, and of course, wine made from pomegranates and grapes. Also on the table would be dates, figs, and honey.

Feasting was a time of celebration and rejoicing. Some feasts were tied to the agricultural year and others celebrated a victory or an historical event. Passover is perhaps the feast in the Old Testament with which we are most familiar. Originally an agricultural event recognizing the spring equinox, it became historically important because of its connection to the Hebrew exodus from Egypt. Passover began at sunset on the evening before the actual feast began. The Passover meal was the first in the week, each day of which there were morning and evening sacrifices. These began with the burning of incense, followed by a burnt offering for the sins of the nation as a whole, and then an offering for the Emperor, and finally private offerings. Thousands of Passover lambs would be offered at exactly half past one o'clock. As evening came on, the lamb designated for a specific family would be roasted. This lamb had to be consumed entirely before midnight.

The New Testament also has many references to food and hospitality. Probably the best-known food story in the Bible is found in all four gospels. This is unusual in itself "(Matthew 14:13-21; Mark 6:30-44; Luke 9:10-17; John 6:1-15). Jesus had been mobbed by crowds, and He withdrew to a boat, but the crowd still followed Him. Time was passing and several of the disciples approached Him urging that He send the crowds away so that the people could get to the villages and buy some food. He told them not to send the people away, but instead, give them something to eat. They replied that they had only five loaves of bread and two fish. Jesus told them to bring the bread and fish to Him, and directed the people to sit down on the grass.

Looking up towards heaven, He gave thanks and then took the fish and the loaves. He directed the disciples to distribute this to the people until they were all satisfied. Even then there were twelve baskets of broken pieces left over. The Bible tells us that the number who ate was 5,000 men, and later women and children. Surely this must mean that as many as 8,000 were fed that day. Jesus used food to show that He and his Father care for us and provide for us, and church food service people do the same today. On a less serious note, today they also may wish they could perform similar miracles. Often they do.

When Jesus had fasted for forty days and forty nights in

the desert, the devil approached him realizing that He was hungry. The devil taunted Him trying to use Jesus' hunger as a wedge to corrupt him. Satan told Jesus that if He was indeed the Son of God why didn't He just turn stones to bread? He was saying, "Enjoy your meal, for you have already done your sacrifice. No harm in doing this; it would not be a spiritual matter." In Matthew 4:4 Jesus responds that man does not live by bread alone. This is another powerful reference using food imagery as an immediately-identifiable way to a larger truth. Artists of the middle ages often depicted ogres devouring the damned in Hell after they had been roasted and boiled, thus continuing the association between Satan, temptation, and eating.

In Matthew 25:35 Jesus speaks to the Disciples about giving Him water when He was thirsty and food when He was hungry. They are puzzled and ask Him when did they ever give Him food or drink. His response is timeless, "Whatever you do for one of the least of these you do for Me." There is surely a modern parallel for each of us and for each church in these words. We show hospitality to those in need as well as to our own church family. This aspect of the modern church kitchen has become a larger mission of the whole church that we will look at in more detail later.

Zaccheus, the unpopular tax collector, learned a lesson when Jesus chose to go to his house rather than that of one of the priests or scribes. Luke tells another favorite parable (Luke 15:11-31) about the son who wanted to take his inheritance and go into the world on his own. Squandering his fortune, he found himself feeding pigs; they were unclean animals and for a Jew to lower himself by doing this

16

was the ultimate humiliation. He wished he had at least as good to eat himself as he was feeding to the pigs. He understood how foolish he had been, and returned to his home. His father promptly welcomed him back with a feast, and served him the famous fatted calf. Here is another instance where food played a vital role in solving human distress and in teaching a life lesson. Once again, celebrating and food were tied together.

Another instance of hospitality with which we are familiar involves Mary and Martha. Luke tells us in Chapter 10:38-41 that Jesus came to the village of Bethany not far from Jerusalem where Mary and Martha lived with Lazarus, their brother. They opened their home to Him as church doors are open to all. Mary sat enthralled at Jesus' feet and listened to his teachings, while Martha fussed about making necessary preparations for the visit. Eventually, Martha became angry that Mary was not helping her, and she asked Jesus to tell Mary to help her with the work. She finds it hard to separate work from being hospitable. Mary needed Jesus; Martha thought that Jesus needed her. Mary thought that Jesus had come to their home to be served, but Martha realized that Jesus had come to save them from sin. Jesus' reply to Martha reminds us that hospitality is more far-reaching than household chores. He urges us to keep focused on the larger issue when He says, "Martha, Martha, you are worried and upset about many things, but only one thing is needed." Important here is that both women loved Jesus although they had very different styles of expressing this love. We are cautioned not to allow serving to become self-serving.

It isn't called The Last Get Together, is it? Or the last staff meeting? In thinking about this amazing event it is reasonable to assume that a meal preceded the serving of the first communion. All of the famous paintings depict the disciples in a banquet setting rather than kneeling. In Matthew we are told that Jesus was "reclining at the table with the twelve" (Matthew 26:20), and it was while they were eating that He spoke of His coming betrayal and death. So Jesus chose to give this momentous information in a food service setting. There is no more significant statement anywhere about the important role food plays in the church.

Meditation: The term fellowship means the expressing of Christian love, particularly in a worship setting. It also means the reception of the sacraments, and refers to simple social occasions such as meals at the church, or playing basketball, or physical work like building Habitat For Humanity houses. In the New Testament this is called *koinona,* which is far more than friendship or good rapport. It is more than the good morale of a close-knit group. Common participation beginning in the church dining hall can be the springboard to *koinona.*

Communion is more than bread and wine. Communion means the coming together of God's people whether it is two or three who are gathered or more. From the beginning eating together has brought people into His house, and we celebrate this whenever we are together, and in whatever room of the church. Here is the Prayer of John Chrysostom from The United Methodist Hymnal 23rd printing, 2001:

"Almighty God,
You have given us grace at this time
With one accord to make our common supplication to you;
And you have promised through your well-beloved Son
That when two or three are gathered together in his name,
You will be in the midst of them."

In our modern times gathering embraces hospitality. Hospitality becomes a mission field, its volunteers having an unusual opportunity to bring people to Christ and His church. People will respond to the offer of a cup of coffee or a meal at the church when they might be reluctant to accept an invitation to worship. Food service is not the end goal of a church, but it surely is a significant part of its beginnings and continuings. What begins in the kitchen spreads throughout the church, its aromas beckoning.

Chapter 2
In the Beginning

Luke:1-3 "Therefore, since I have investigated everything, it seemed good also to write an orderly account for you."

The psalmist tells us (Psalm 111:7-8) that the precepts of the Lord are steadfast forever and ever, and that they are trustworthy. This idea has built many strong churches, and although they have different beginnings, their similarities are more significant.

Then...and Now

Peachtree Road United Methodist
Atlanta, Georgia

In January of 1925 a survey by the Sunday School Board and a group of Emory University theology students revealed a need for a Methodist church in what was then a rural area of Atlanta called "Buckhead." A group of 19 persons committed to establishing a new church there. By June there were 80 members who signed a note enabling the purchase of property on Peachtree Road. The structure erected there had a roof and a ceiling but no walls. As the years passed the church had financial troubles and was saved from foreclosure by a substantial donation from Emory University. Within the year it moved about a block, and began building and acquiring additional property. 1 Today there are 7,500 members and multiple buildings.

Remember your church hostess? Definitely a she, and likely 60 years older or more. She was a member of the congregation, and probably one day volunteered to serve lunch for the women's group of which she was a member. Someone had donated their existing stove when they moved to a new house, and so the lunch was prepared at the church. Then another group asked for her help, and another, and eventually the church decided to pay her for her services. Her job description called her Church Hostess. Such was the beginning of church food service shortly after the end of

World War II at Peachtree Road United Methodist Church with Mary Stewart as hostess. Mary served in this capacity until 1975 when she was in her 80s.

It is interesting to note here that as men came into church food service in the 1990s none of them was ever called "host." Certainly we could speculate about how this happened, but it would be an omission not to point out that "hostess" refers to females only and that this title tends to undervalue their position on the church staff, even if not intentionally. It has been said, "If you are female, wear an apron, and work in the kitchen it is hard for the staff and the congregation to take you seriously." It is a fact that some church hostesses were not permitted to attend staff meetings although events that directly concerned them were discussed and planned there. Many church hostesses had known for a long time that their family was dependent upon their income, but it took the arrival of men in this same job to raise both its status and its salary. And women were grateful for this even though it happened without their leadership.

Times were less hectic in the 1940s and 50s, and this noble lady could juggle family and home pretty well. Mary Stewart never used prepared foods; her chicken salad and homemade pies were legendary. The dishes she served all came from her personal recipe file. As hostess she also arranged flowers for special events, and regularly checked the pulpit for dust or scratches. Anyone who assisted her was a volunteer, most likely her friend. And for a lot of years this and the covered dish dinner comprised church food service, not just at this church, but at virtually all churches.

Gradually the job which had been occasional became daily, and the home-style stove became inadequate. Our noble lady encountered her limitations.

Peachtree Road Methodist now has a staff of six who serve not only their church but the community as well. Just a bit later current Food Service Director Al McDaniel who is a classically trained chef, will share some interesting thoughts about challenges he faces.

It is probably well to digress a moment here to talk about covered-dish or pot luck dinners. There are three things that can happen at a covered-dish dinner, and two of them are bad. Usually there are lots of green beans and rolls, and not much in the way of entrees. A lovely lady comes in with four blueberry muffins, but eats dinner. To her way of thinking four muffins is a lot, much more than she would ever eat, but for a family of four, those muffins don't even begin to cover their plates.

So, to have a successful covered-dish dinner, ask everyone to bring 12 servings. Go alphabetically by last name and assign the dishes that way. A through E brings vegetables, F through J brings desserts and so on. Try to assign entrees to the span of the alphabet that has the most participants, usually M through T. This can be rotated if there are frequent covered-dish dinners. It is important to know who will provide tea and coffee.

And finally ask participants to consider the equipment available in the kitchen. If everybody brings something that has to go in the oven there will be big delays. It is also essential to hold back some of the dishes rather than putting everything out at once. If that happens, diners consider this a huge smorgasbord, and all the food disappears rapidly, leaving those at the end of the line with the green beans and rolls. Some churches provide purchased fried chicken and guests bring the rest. It's also really neat to ask families to provide recipes of the favorite dishes they bring.

First Baptist
Tyler, Texas

The American south was first in organized church food service and dominates it today. It evolved rather than was created, and eventually the idea spread to many states. It just came to be, and a lot of structure today traces to these early beginnings. First Baptist in Tyler, Texas was founded in 1848 by 8 people who got together in the log courthouse. They were the fifty-third Baptist congregation to be organized in Texas. Their first building was erected in 1855, and since then the church has built multiple times. Food service began in a remodeled area of the church in 1939 with covered dish dinners. Today its professional staff serves about 300 persons on Wednesday nights, offering a choice between two entrees, a baked potato bar, and several side dishes. Usually there are three different desserts, one of which is sugar free.

An interesting current innovation is their Ninos de Promesa, a program whose purpose is to prepare Hispanic children for public school. Understanding that nutrition is crucial to brain development in preschool children, food service personnel have assisted in creating breakfasts, lunches, and snacks which teach children (and their parents through take-home menus) good eating habits that the church hopes will become a lifestyle.

First Baptist now has a south campus where an additional hundred persons are served each Wednesday. This is an example of another modern trend in church food service where the original church creates satellite locations like this one in Tyler. This south campus is 150 acres and about 10 miles from the parent church. Teri Sawyer, food service director, manages both locations and has recently written a cookbook, *Delicious By Design*, featuring some of her favorite recipes and telling about the journey which led her to First Baptist.

Los Altos United Methodist
Los Altos, California

Quite different in its beginnings is Los Altos United Methodist Church in Los Altos, California. It started under an apricot orchard in 1952 with 50-60 people. Today its joined buildings spread out rather than rise high over about four acres. It somewhat resembles a retreat center or spa in appearance. They are California-style in all they do: menus, campus, and method of service. They have a cookout once a week using volunteers at the grills and at the serving tables as well. There is entertainment at each of these cookouts. Los Altos has a lot of special meals such as a Valentine Party, men's breakfasts, and a free Thanksgiving dinner. Ellie Manser, food service manager at Los Altos, also has initiated a central store where church members can purchase paper goods and coffee-related items at her cost. Seasonal gift baskets are another of Ellie's projects.

Ben Hill United Methodist
Atlanta, Georgia

In 1853 a Mr. Sidney Robins donated a tract of land for the establishment of a new congregation. A log cabin was built on this site and was the first building for the new church. It was part of a four-circuit, meaning they had a minister only once a month. In 1875 the church was relocated to Mt. Gilead Campground, and named Wesley Chapel Methodist Church.

After the Civil War Mt. Gilead got its own post office. It was named after Benjamin Harvey Hill, the new senator from Georgia, and a great orator of his day. The church thrived and by 1930 a basement had been dug, and church schoolrooms were added. The church was renamed Ben Hill Methodist Church, and its growth continued through the 1940s, 1950s, and 1960s.

Prior to 1970 Ben Hill was an all-white middle class congregation of several thousand. It was a time when Atlanta was changing and when neighborhoods were changing also. Middle class black families moved into the area, and by 1975 the Methodist Bishop recognized the changing dynamics and appointed an African American to serve as Ben Hill's senior pastor.

In the summer of 1980 Atlanta experienced what we have come to call the cases of the "missing and murdered children." Visited solely upon the black community, it was a time of national attention and local fear. Children who had been allowed to play outside or on playgrounds or vacant lots were kept home by their parents who were terrified for their safety. Nowhere was there a safe place for these children, and so the parents turned to their church for help. Ben Hill responded to this crisis by instigating a summer camp for any child who wished to come. Where there are kids all day long, there has got to be food, and so Annie Laura Stephens was selected as cook for summer camp. She remembers being paid $75 a week for her work. This was the beginning of food service at Ben Hill.

The congregation continued to occupy the same buildings, and the same kitchen. Food service was mostly "pot luck," except for various receptions which were managed by volunteers and offered free to the congregation. They remain so to this day, the church absorbing all costs for these functions. These receptions honor various people for outstanding achievements, or celebrate church occasions and national holidays. It has not been unusual to serve 800 or more people at one of these events. This represents a sizeable financial commitment by the church.

When Wednesday night suppers began Annie Laura was once again called into service. She has continued to serve her church through these years as both volunteer and staff member.

Prestonwood Baptist
Plano, Texas

This church began in February of 1977 in Dallas, services being held initially at a local park's recreation center. In 1983 the congregation occupied a new 4,000-seat worship center. By the close of the 1980s the then membership of 11,000 had also outgrown that facility, and shortly thereafter they moved to their current location in Plano. In May of 1999 Prestonwood occupied its 7,000-seat worship center. Today's membership at Prestonwood is in excess of 28,000 persons.

Food service began about 2002, Aramark Catering Service being awarded the contract. After two and a half years the church assumed the ministry of food service, and employed Eddy Espinosa to be its director. Currently Eddy operates out of 3 different kitchens; he has a staff of 45 with an additional 40 who are "on call." The food service budget is 2.1 million dollars that includes daily meals for the 1,500 students in the school. All in all about 400,000 meals are served each year.

Eddy says that the heart of his food ministry is good service that touches lives and reaches people through the very practical, everyday thing like eating. He says that as churches grow they offer more ministry programs on campus, nearly all of which require food in one form or another. He uses trinity-usa.net for a good bit of his purchasing, because it has no up front cost to the church. This is a cooperative purchasing organization which utilizes volume as a tool to keep prices low. 2

Every Sunday Prestonwood offers selections from six food stations in the Main Street Café: a salad bar, a Starbucks, a pizza made on site in wood-burning ovens, a world station featuring various different cuisines each week, a home cooking station, and a sizzle station.

Eddy believes that as they invite people to stay after worship he needs to offer them a warm place to hang out, enjoy their friends and build relationships.

Myers Park Presbyterian Church
Charlotte, North Carolina

In 1926 a group of local leaders, meeting at the Chamber of Commerce and other locations in suburban Charlotte, focused on a need for a Presbyterian church. As a result of these meetings Myers Park Presbyterian was formed and became the twenty-second Presbyterian church in the area. Four officers were elected and they addressed the need for a minister and a building. The first worship service occurred in the new sanctuary on April 7, 1929. It came to be known as Unit #1 on the church's building program. 3

It took 50 years for the church to have an organized food service department. During some of those years a cook named Magnolia prepared meals for church events. Her recipes were delicious, but also very secret. She was followed by a caterer named Todd Townsend in the late '80s, but as his own business grew he was forced to give up his work at Myers Park. Then came a succession of caterers and volunteers, during which time a volunteer named Wendy Kenney organized a cookbook called *Count Our Blessings* in honor of the church's 75th anniversary. It was a very successful publication. Wendy continues as a volunteer today and assists in various food functions.

Finally a new minister coming to Myers Park brought with him a commitment to establish a real food service department. He authorized a major clean-up of the kitchen facility as well as purchase of some new equipment. Mimi Rees was hired in 2004 and is there today. There is an outreach program called "Room At The Inn" where about 15 homeless persons sleep overnight at the church. Three volunteers pick them up, stay with them overnight, and return them by van the next morning. This is a Charlotte city-wide program.

The Changes

Food has been neglected as a topic of study or investigation previously because most people take it for granted. After all each one of us eats, and by virtue of this activity, we may have assumed therefore that we knew all we needed to know about eating. Personal preference seemed to be all the information needed. Everybody has cooked something at one time or another, and so food preparation is a topic about which many consider themselves expert.

Today there is much awareness of the growing, harvesting, and preparation of foods. In the past most of the food eaten was either grown on the family's own farm or that of their neighbor, but the advent of better growing methods, overnight transportation, canning, refrigeration, and freezing have produced a revolution in the availability of foodstuffs. Probably the disappearance of the family kitchen garden occurred when frozen vegetables and large chain grocery stores appeared, and although this was a welcome convenience, it did limit available ingredients, sometimes rendering them tasteless. Some viewed this as a victory of quantity over quality.

In the past several hundred years there has been a great change in our attitudes about food and the table where it is served. We have noted that dining occurred anywhere a tablecloth was laid, and was easily facilitated since utensils and bowls were shared (1), the food being placed strategically between several persons. After the appearance of the dining room and dining table, gatherings for political and social reasons started a long upward journey of importance.

Originally the church was not only the center of worship but also the center of social events. Lack of transportation contributed to the centralization of life at the church. There weren't any malls or movie houses or gathering places or anywhere else church members could have refreshments and visit with neighbors in a social setting. Teens met their boyfriends/girlfriends at church for sock hops and seasonal events.

Not only has the role of the church changed over the years, so has their member, and dramatically. Originally most folks who ate at church probably walked there, living close to where they worshipped. Pretty close to 100% of the women were not employed—if they were it was as teachers, nurses, or librarians—and the thought of eating out was very appealing. The husbands were probably home by 5:30pm, and they too were glad to go to the church and see friends. The kids loved another opportunity to play with their schoolmates. If there was TV its broadcast hours and number of channels was very limited. There was no internet. Vacations were likely to a spot within easy driving distance in the one car the family owned. There wasn't much in the way of organized sports for kids.

Today's church family is vastly different. Likely 50+% of the mothers work outside the home, and so, rather than being glad for an evening out, after work they have errands to do while the kids are at soccer or choir practice. The dads are little league coaches, or scout leaders if they don't have late business meetings. Only a very small percentage of large-church members live within walking distance of their church; some actually have a 45-minute commute utilizing crowded freeways. Thus there is a trend towards Sunday lunches and events, although in most churches it is in-addition-to rather than instead-of the mainstay Wednesday night supper. Wednesday night suppers now have three main constituencies: seniors, young marrieds, and singles, although some families continue to be a part of this event.

The technology age has brought wireless everything and immediate access to the web not only for the adults but for the kids as well. Adults and kids are technically sophisticated today in ways never imagined earlier. This and extended travel have changed the palate of the diner. Whereas fresh asparagus was once a gourmet treat at church, now the customer has had French food in Paris, pasta in Italy, and enchiladas in Mexico. They expect more of an upgraded menu featuring exotic food or other continental dishes, and always steamed fresh vegetables.

Nutritional Needs

Another modern trend in church food service is the customers' concern about health and nutrition. They want less fat, less salt, and fewer "bubbling caldrons" in the kitchen. Those green beans should stay green and crisp; the same is true of other vegetables as well. Salt, sugar, and fat are used sparingly, and although they are not dieticians, today's food service directors are called upon to consider special dietary needs and other personal preferences. There are many, many more challenges to church kitchens today than ever before. Because of the close and personal relationship between members and their church, expectations exist here that are not present at local restaurants. Here are those relative comments from Al McDaniel:

"Menu planning is by far the most difficult aspect of my job, because of comments and requests I hear weekly. Vegetarians want more vegetarian friendly meals, but if I don't serve meat I will hear that I served a "cheap" meal. Some members do not eat pork and want alternative entrees when pork chops, pork loin, or barbecue are served. Others ask for a non-red meat option or for a non-fried entrée when a fried entrée is on the menu. There are requests now for Weight Watcher menus with their points posted alongside. Seniors want substantial lunches as this will be their main meal of the day, but others prefer lighter fare at noon. The old standby casserole is regarded with disdain. Everyone wants delicious desserts which have hardly any sugar or fat but taste the same as those that do."

All of this calls for more education, more training, and more patience on the part of the food service staff. Where a diner wouldn't dream of entering the kitchen at a local restaurant, they feel perfectly free to do so at their church. This is both an advantage and a disadvantage.

An excellent source of information is the National Association of Church Food Service (www.nacfs.org; 404-261-1794), comprised of members throughout the United States. With an annual educational conference and local chapters, NACFS offers the opportunity for interaction with food service directors. Few have ever had a chance to talk with a genuine colleague.

No matter how well intentioned, church staff members do not have the expertise to make informed food service recommendations and decisions. They are often put in a position to be expert about these matters—food service directors typically report to the business administrator—but these persons' training and experience do not, nor is it intended to,enable them to make complicated food service decisions. Thus a large void can be created between those who do the work and those who may make decisions about it. This is when the doctrine of unintended consequences may play a major role.

Church Facilities

People are not all that has changed at America's churches; the buildings have become mega complexes in some cases and updated in almost all others. The kitchen that started with that donated stove now likely has tilt skillets, steamers, convection ovens, and walk-in coolers and freezers. Not all churches have all these items, but most have at least some of them. Fellowship halls have been added, some with enormous seating capacity, and the frequency of meal requests has increased as the congregation has grown. It is a mistake to think that the fine service Mary Stewart gave would even begin to satisfy congregations of the 2000s.

Meditation: Having reverence for history and keeping an orderly account of it compels us to respect the present. Particularly we are indebted to those who serve in less-obvious ways. Not as visible as the choir or clergy, kitchen staff and volunteers work just as surely for the kingdom.

Chapter 3
The 5,000 Were Fed Only Once

1 Timothy 4:15 "Be diligent in these matters;
give yourself wholly to them so that everyone may see your progress."

God pays attention to those who call on him. Sometimes it is escape from trouble; sometimes it is help in times of trouble. In Matthew 22:1-10 Jesus tells the parable of the wedding feast. A king prepared a wedding feast for his son, and sent invitations to his friends and significant officials. But they did not come. Some went to their businesses, some went to their fields, some were too busy to attend. The king said to his servants, "Those I invited did not deserve to come. Go to the street corners and invite anyone you find whether they are good or bad." And the wedding hall was filled with guests.

Many of His blessings require active participation and the following stories are about this.

Serving the Homeless

First United Methodist
Gastonia, North Carolina

This church has an interesting approach to feeding the homeless. Twice a year they have a soup kitchen, but the customers are not usually the homeless, although they are welcome. The audience served is the local townspeople who come to eat soups and chili at the church. The minimum cost for the eat-as-much-as-you-want lunch is $5.00 but diners are encouraged to contribute more. This fund-raising event benefits the shelters for battered women and the homeless. All food is donated; all supplies are furnished by the church, and so what is collected goes directly back into the needs of the community.

This is an anticipated event held in September and February each year. Gastonians go not only to participate in this outreach but also for the hearty food. Under the direction of Linda Nolen, food service director, soups and other menu items are served. Local restaurants donate food, the church kitchen cooks it or keeps it hot and serves beverages. Favorite soups are cream of broccoli, potato, mushroom, won ton, chili, Brunswick stew, and of course vegetable. Local ladies' groups make cakes and cookies for dessert. It is always well-attended by people from all walks of life and all denominations.

An additional part of First Methodist's outreach is a weekly breakfast. Served at the Salvation Army facility, churches in the area each have an assigned day to prepare breakfast for the homeless. This is a once-a-week, 52 times a year commitment.

St. Luke's Episcopal
Atlanta, Georgia

St. Luke's Episcopal began in the early 1900s in the heart of what was then a neighborhood of Atlanta,Georgia's most-elegant homes. It was built of the finest materials, and featured 19 stained-glass windows (not all completed initially) that are even today famous for their rich, deep purples and intense reds and golds. The windows were restored in 1992. Today St. Luke's stands in the heart of the downtown area, with tall office buildings, Centennial Park, and the Civic Center as its neighbors.

In 1974 one of the church members wanted to help a person who came to the church door. She made him a sandwich; he told several of his friends, and they came with him the next time. Out of this single sandwich the St. Luke's Community Kitchen was born under the direction of that woman, Jenny Pierson. She got volunteers to make soup and sandwiches at their homes and bring them to the church each noon.

Soon the Community Kitchen became an on-going part of the parish, and what had begun as lunch for 20 to 30 people was a table for 75-100 people. It was affectionately called "Luke's Place." In 1981 the church hired a director and added a cook to prepare the food for the 450 persons who came each day. Several years later the soup kitchen was actually added as an item to the church budget and a long-range planning committee was established.

There were numerous volunteers who came to assist in cooking and serving. A lot of these initial volunteers continue to work today, many of them having served for 10 years or longer. There is one person who began by helping Jenny, and now at 85 years of age she continues her faithful service weekly. It is interesting that the Atlanta Community Food Bank actually started at St. Luke's as an outgrowth of their Community Kitchen.

In 1997 the St. Luke's Community Kitchen became Crossroads Community Ministries and Clyde Corbin was hired as Food Service Manager. At this time with a grant from United Parcel Service and funds raised by the church, a building was remodeled and furnished with commercial kitchen equipment. The new CCM occupied this space and remains there today. In these years Clyde has served over 2 and one-quarter million meals, and his welcoming smile, joy of spirit, and cooking skills are known to all. He has about sixty volunteers who help in the kitchen, usually 10 per day.

Frequently the menu is determined by donations from Atlanta's Table (leftover food from high-end eateries), Publix Grocery Stores, and Old Fashioned Foods. This company by itself donates about 9,000 pounds of food each month. The state government assists financially, and groups like Candler School of Theology, Columbia Theological Seminary, Georgia State University, the University of Georgia, and Leadership Atlanta collaborate in making this ministry possible. All of these join together with St. Luke's and private donations to insure the continuation of the program.

The food is but part of the larger CCM mission. Witness this statement from Robert T. Lind, Chair: "When I first joined the CCM board I was a "skeptic." Homelessness to me was just a bunch of people with no direction—people who didn't care about themselves or Atlanta, and who had little, if any, support from the community.

"Well, I was wrong from many perspectives. My view was they should stop moping around, get focused, and get a job.

"But that was easier said than done. Since being on the CCM board and working more closely with the challenge of homelessness and poverty, I've come to somewhat of an awakening about what can be done and what we need to do. There are those who say these folks don't need help because they won't help themselves, but I've learned otherwise. There is something that we can do about the cycle of homelessness and poverty.

"Crossroads provides a great starting point. Our mission is focused on getting those who want it into training and assistance programs which will prepare them to re-enter the workforce. We want them to earn a living, find a home and regain their lives as productive citizens." 4

The Reverend Dan Matthews of St. Luke's describes CCM as "having respect for the humanity of each and every person who finds themselves on the street. Our ministry is a form of respect that invites people to be involved in their own solutions. It is a form of respect that invites people to avail themselves of the opportunities offered to them by Crossroads Community Ministries. Our clients are invited to view themselves not as the world has judged them, but as we here view them—as worthy of respect and full of potential." 4

So, while food and fellowship is not the whole essence of CCM, it is the bridge to something larger. Recently, in cooperation with the Waffle House restaurant chain, Clyde Corbin has been training apprentices in food service. At the completion of their training they are given a permanent job at the restaurant. A number of his graduates have been on their job for 8 or more years. Clyde says that 90% of the persons who come to eat have no I.D, no social security card, no birth certificate, and no address. CCM will help them acquire the first three items, and provides them with the fourth. The church maintains a post office where over 2,000 persons receive mail and which they may list as their permanent address. There is a clinic each day with trained professionals who can help with minor health problems or make referrals to a hospital for major ones. On Saturdays other churches in the area provide breakfast and Bible study for about 125 persons.

St. Luke's Episcopal may not be the usual example of serving the homeless, but it certainly shows what a church and a congregation that is dedicated to a specific mission can accomplish.

Meals on Wheels

Today's mobile nutrition programs in the United States trace their roots back to Great Britain during World War II (1939). During the blitz when Germany daily bombed England, many people lost their homes and therefore their ability to cook for themselves. A volunteer group responded to this emergency by preparing and delivering meals to their neighbors. This same group also took refreshments to servicemen in canteens; these deliveries came to be known as "meals on wheels."

Following the war the United States started its own experimental meal program. It began as a single small group serving seven seniors, and today serves hundreds of thousands of elderly, disabled, or at-risk persons across the country. The first organized American home-delivered meal program (that was not church sponsored) began in Philadelphia, Pennsylvania in January of 1954. It was funded by a grant from a local foundation, and aimed at providing nourishment that met the dietary needs of homebound seniors and other shut-ins. As is the case today many of the recipients do not need medical supervision, but simply a helping hand in order to maintain their independence.

In an effort both to cover costs and to maintain the recipient's sense of dignity, the program charged a fee ranging from $.40 t $ 80 per day. No one was refused because of inability to pay, and the fee could be adjusted based upon the individual's circumstances. The Visiting Nurse Society and the Philadelphia Department of Public

Assistance were used to refer potential clients. Another successful method of identifying eligible members was through concerned neighbors or family who provided names of those who might benefit from delivered meals.

Columbus, Ohio was the second city in the United States to establish a community-based meals program. Building on the Philadelphia model, a federation of local women's clubs provided a list of possible participants for meals. After identifying a prospective client, a member from one of the women's clubs would visit the person on the list, evaluating his/her ability to pay for meals, and the need for them. The sliding fee scale was from $.80 to $2.00 a day. In Columbus all meals were prepared by local restaurants and delivered by taxi cabs on weekdays and by high school students on weekends.

Rochester, New York began its home-delivered meal program in 1958. It too looked to the Visiting Nurse Service as well as to some state agencies for referrals. They also had a sliding scale for their meals ranging from $.50 to $1.85 per meal. Other cities nationwide instituted their own programs, and the mode was set for what we call "meals on wheels." 6

Chillicothe United Methodist
Chillicothe, Ohio

In 1970 Church Women United in Chillicothe, Ohio recognized a local need. One of these women was dietician at Hedrick Medical Center, and therefore had the knowledge as well as the ability to prepare extra meals. On a rotating basis several churches pick the meals up at the hospital and deliver them in insulated carriers. There are 3 Baptist, 1 Presbyterian, 1 Christian, 1 Church of Christ, and this Methodist church which deliver meals. The charge for those who can afford it is $2.50 per meal. They deliver every day including Christmas and Thanksgiving, and maintain a list of who to call in the event no one answers the knock at the door.

Two significant voices in this program are Shirley Tye and Betty Phillips. Betty continues to administer meals on wheels from her residence at Baptist Nursing Home!

Ohio can have really bad winters with snow and sleet and very low temperatures which might seem to cancel the delivery of meals. But no, if the regular drivers cannot make the deliveries, the Rural Electrification Administration does it for them in their specially-equipped vehicles. This represents a real community effort.

Hillside United Methodist
Woodstock, Georgia

Sponsored by Cherokee County Senior Services, Hillside participates in a Meals-on-Wheels program under the direction of staff member Christy Good. Food is received from Bateman Senior Services at two different locations where it is kept hot or cold as stipulated by the Cherokee County Health Department. The meals are then picked-up and delivered by Hillside, Lake Arrowhead Chapel, Hickory Flat United Methodist, First Baptist Churches of Woodstock and Canton, and Waleska United Methodist.

The overall coordinator of this Meals-on-Wheels program is Sharon Smith who has held this position for over 15 years. She believes it had been in existence for 15 prior years before her arrival. They deliver approximately 200 meals a day and are obligated to provide this service for at least 250 days each calendar year. Her two facilities are regularly inspected for cleanliness and for assurance that all equipment is working properly.

Donations by recipients provide a small part of the budget; the major part is funded by the federal government with the state and county also contributing. The time and efforts of the churches and their volunteers enables this program to continue. There is always a waiting list. Probably a large percentage of Meals-on-Wheels throughout the nation is similarly underwritten by a government agency. Sharon is also proud of her "Adopt a Senior" program in which individual recipients are adopted for the Christmas season. Currently there are about 250 of these partners who provide two requested Christmas gifts to the MOW person they have selected.

Hillside United Methodist on its own has a summer lunch program. Children who receive a free lunch during the regular school year need lunch year 'round, and so the church prepares one thousand lunches a week which are distributed to these kids. This unique program is funded and staffed entirely by the church.

Church School Food Service

There are several reasons a church will open a school, but likely the most significant one is that the membership wishes to have their children educated in a Christian environment. In today's world separation of church and state has become a major political issue, and parents resent the state's forbidding of prayer in school and observance of certain Christian holidays.

Discipline of students and dress in public schools also are factors in persuading parents to ask their church to begin a school. It will be a major step for any church, impacting finances, and requiring them to make decisions about the school staff, about after-school activities, choosing curriculum, and available space, all the while maintaining a quality education for students. Not a small part of this scenario is that usually the church Sunday school and the church day school share at least some of the same space. Missing crayons and cleanliness can quickly become a gigantic territorial hassle. School food service is but a part of this, but it is a readily-identifiable complaint venue. Kids probably do not complain about their teacher's ability or curriculum, but they, by golly, will surely voice their dissatisfaction with their lunch to their parents. So, a tip of the hat to church food service directors who are also most often school cafeteria managers.

It is well to note that parochial schools may apply to their state or county for financial assistance, but if granted, the government and its rules and regulations become a large part of the school's operations. Most churches opt out of seeking this assistance even if it means that the church stands ready to cover any losses. Usually the church provides heat, air conditioning, electricity, water, and clean up to the school without charge.

A very helpful website about church schools and camps is healthiergeneration.org. Its purpose is also to encourage healthy eating away from school. There are lots of good ideas here.

Eastside Baptist Church
Roswell, Georgia

This church of about 5,000 members has had an elementary school of 300 students since 1985. Hazel Roll has been cafeteria manager of the school since its inception. When asked what piece of advice she would give another school food service manager embarking on serving students, Hazel immediately replied, "Don't think serving kids will be easy!"

The Eastside School is open to all denominations, or no denomination, with the understanding that all students must participate in daily Bible classes and bi-monthly chapel services. They have kids of different religious backgrounds, and this diversity has not caused problems. We are reminded of this entreaty in Romans 14:1 "Accept him whose faith is weak, without passing judgement on disputable matters."

Eastside must be accredited by the state each year, and is

regularly inspected by the Health Department in order to keep its license. They have a school clinic with a licensed nurse and regularly test student vision and hearing. There are no school busses; all students arrive by carpool and wear uniforms.

Eastside school is designed to be self-supporting, but there are budget subsidies as mentioned above. In the event of a major economic problem which negatively impacts the school the church stands by with financial assistance. They follow the county public school schedule, and a recent spin-off for older students is Dominion High School, housed elsewhere.

Hazel tells about little William who on his first school day was served lasagna which he didn't like. Taking him over the edge was the fact that there was no ice cream; when Hazel consoled him with a kiss, he wiped it off! After a while he came to love Hazel's food, and began calling her a good cook. He said it hardly ever makes him throw up. She now gets cards from the kids asking if they can come live with her. She feels that this part of her ministry is one of the most rewarding things she does. On the next pages are menu samples from the school.

Eastside Christian School Lunch Menu
K-5th grade - $3.50   JANUARY
6th - 8th grades $4.00

MONDAY	TUESDAY	WEDNESDAY	THURSDAY	FRIDAY
7 Grilled Chicken Sandwich; Tater Tots; Salad; Mandarin Oranges	**8** Popcorn Shrimp; Vegetable Fried Rice; Egg rolls; Pineapple rings	**9** Domino's pizza	**10** Hot wings; French fries; Carrot and celery sticks; Jello	**11** Spaghetti With Meat Sauce; Green Beans; Garlic Bread; Ice Cream
Soup (Salad bar); Turkey & cheese sandwich (brown bag)	Grilled chicken (salad bar); Turkey & cheese sandwich (brown bag)		Soup (Salad Bar); Turkey and cheese sandwich (brown bag)	Chicken salad (salad bar); Turkey & cheese sandwich (brown bag)
14 Chicken Noodle Soup; Grilled Cheese Sandwich; Peach Halves	**15** Country Fried Steak; Mashed Potatoes; Green Beans; Rolls	**16** Domino's pizza	**17** Cheeseburger; Potato Wedges; Carrot Sticks w/ Ranch Dressing; Ice Cream	**18** Mexican Chilupitos; Rice; Chips & Cheese; Cinnamon applesauce
Grilled chicken (salad bar); Ham & cheese sandwich (brown bag)	Ham cubes (salad bar); Ham & cheese sandwich (brown bag)		Chicken salad (salad bar); Ham & cheese sandwich (brown bag)	Potato Bar (salad bar); Ham & cheese sandwich (brown bag)
21 Hot Dogs; Potato Wedges; Carrot sticks w/ ranch dressing; Apples	**22** Ham and Cheese Sandwich; Assorted Potato Chips; Carrots with Ranch Dressings; Fruit	**23** Domino's pizza	**24** Grilled Chicken Sandwich; Tater Tots; Salad; Chocolate Pudding	**25** Little Charlies Pizza; Salad; Ice Cream
(Soup) Salad Bar; Peanut butter & Jelly (Brown bag)	(Tuna Salad) Salad Bar; Peanut butter & Jelly (brown bag)		(Grilled Chicken) Salad Bar; Peanut butter & Jelly (brown bag)	No Salad Bar; Peanut Butter & Jelly (brown bag)
28 Sweet & Sour Shrimp; Steamed Rice; Mandarin Vegetables; Pineapple Chunks	**29** Nachos Supreme; Spanish Rice; Refried Beans; Ice Cream	**30** Domino's	**31** Chicken Alfredo; Linguine Noodles; Steamed Vegetables; Garlic Toast; Peach Halves	
Baked Potato Salad; Turkey And Cheese Sandwich	(Tuna Salad) Salad Bar; Turkey And Cheese Sandwich		(Soup) Salad Bar; Turkey Sandwich (Brown Bag)	
31				

Salad Bar is an **ALTERNATE** lunch choice for grades 6th-8th **ONLY**. Every day salad bar will include the item above in "gray", plus lettuce, tomato, cucumber, olives, eggs, bell pepper, bacon bits, croutons, pudding or Jell-O. Brown bag (another alternate choice for K-8) will include an item in "gray", chips, apple & cookie. MILK is included with hot lunch, salad bar and brown bag lunch. Additional milk will be $.50 if also available at a (tempting) lunch from home. ICE CREAM will be an additional charge of $.50 unless listed with your menu choice. Ice cream will only be available to buy when listed on the menu.

How to fill out the envelope: Place a checkmark in the box for the day you are choosing hot lunch, place an "A" in the box for the brown bag lunch, and an "S" if you are choosing salad bar (6th-8th only).

Please make your check payable to **EASTSIDE BAPTIST CHURCH**, not the school.
Lunch money is due to your Homeroom Teacher by Friday, September 21, 2007.

Eastside Christian School Lunch Menu
NOVEMBER 2007

K - 5th grade - $3.50   6th – 8th grade - $4.00

MONDAY	TUESDAY	WEDNESDAY	THURSDAY	FRIDAY
Potato Bar (salad bar) Turkey & Cheese sandwich (brown bag)	Grilled Chicken (salad bar) Turkey & Cheese sandwich (brown bag)		Hot wings French Fries Carrot and Celery Sticks Jello 1	Spaghetti w/ Meat Sauce Green Beans Garlic Bread Ice Cream 2
5 Hot Dog Bar Chili, Shredded Cheese Fries Cole Slaw Ice Cream	6 Grilled Chicken Sandwich Tater Tots Lettuce/Pickle/Tomato Mandarin Oranges	7 Nachos Pizza	8 Country Fried Steak Mashed Potatoes w/ Gravy Green Peas Brownie	9 Chicken Salad (salad bar) Turkey & Cheese sandwich (brown bag) — Mexican Chimizpizo Rice Chips & Cheese Cinnamon Applesauce
12 Grilled Chicken (salad bar) Ham & Cheese sandwich (brown bag) — Cheeseburger Potato Wedges Carrot Sticks w/ Ranch Dressing Apples	13 Ham Cubes (salad bar) Ham & Cheese sandwich (brown bag) — Sweet & Sour Chicken Steamed Rice Mandarin Vegetables Pineapple Chunks	14 Deannes Pizza	15 Chicken Salad (salad bar) Ham & Cheese sandwich (brown bag) — Chicken Filet Sandwich Lettuce/Tomato Chips Applesauce	16 Potato Bar (salad bar) Ham & Cheese sandwich (brown bag) — Scrambled Eggs Bacon Grits Biscuits And Gravy
19 Chicken Salad (salad bar) Peanut Butter & Jelly (brown bag) — THANKSGIVING WEEK	20 Potato Bar (salad bar) Peanut Butter & Jelly (brown bag) — NO SCHOOL	21 W/B R/PEE	22 Grilled Chicken (salad bar) Peanut Butter & Jelly (brown bag) — ENJOY	23 Ham cubes (salad bar) Peanut Butter & Jelly (brown bag) — SEE YOU MONDAY
26 Ham, Cheese & Salami Sandwich Chips Carrot Sticks w/ Ranch Dressing Fruit	27 Chicken Tenders Mac and Cheese Mixed Veggies Brownies	28 Deannes Pizza	29 Spaghetti Meat Sauce Salad Garlic Bread Fruit	30 Nachos Supreme Spanish Rice Refried Beans Ice Cream
Chicken Salad (salad bar)	Potato Bar (salad bar)		Grilled Chicken (salad bar)	Ham Cubes (salad bar)

Salad Bar is an ALTERNATE lunch choice for grades 6 - 8 ONLY. Every day salad bar will include the item above in "gray" plus lettuce, tomato, cucumber, olives, eggs, bell pepper, bacon bits, croutons, pudding or J-ell-O. Brown Bag (another alternate choice for K-8) will include item in "gray" plus chips, apple & cookie. Milk is included with hot lunch, salad bar and brown bag lunch. Additional milk will be $.50 also available when bringing lunch from home) ICE CREAM will be an additional charge of $.50 unless printed with your menu choice. Ice cream will only be available to buy when listed on the menu.

How to fill out the envelope: Place a check for the day you are choosing hot lunch, place an "A" in the box for the brown bag lunch and an "S" if you are choosing salad bar (6 - 8 only).

Please make your check payable to EASTSIDE BAPTIST CHURCH, not the school.

Lunch money is due to your Homeroom Teacher by Friday, September 21, 2007.

Roswell Street Baptist
Marietta, Georgia

Susan Orr, former Food Service Director, tells of the twelve years her church had a school.

They served babies aged 6 months and up in the child development center, and went through grade 8 in the school. As their congregation outgrew the existing fellowship hall and occupied a new facility, the school inherited the old space for meals and other activities.

The school was never intended to be completely self-supporting. In addition to the less obvious things like heat and lights and insurance, the church budget regularly contributed 25% of the school's expenses, more if needed. At the time the school was operating, the students paid $2 per meal. Snacks were served twice daily. On the next pages are menu selections from Roswell Street.

February 2003

Lunch Menu

Monday	Tuesday	Wednesday	Thursday	Friday
3 Hamburger/Bun Sweet potato fries Peas & Carrots Peaches Chocolate Chip Cookie Milk	**4** Beef Stew Yellow rice Apples/Applesauce Lima beans Cheesy Roll Milk	**5** Zesty Ravioli Corn-on-the-cob/ creamed corn Green beans Orange Wedge Garlic Bread Milk	**6** Chicken Nuggets Creamed potatoes Broccoli & cheese Roll Strawberry jell-o Milk	**7** Potato Skins w/ cheese & bacon Green beans Pineapple Roll Chocolate ice cream cups Milk
10 Tomato soup or Chicken noodle soup Grilled cheese sandwich Broccoli, cauliflower, & carrot medley Peaches Oyster crackers Milk	**11** Turkey & gravy Cornbread dressing Green beans Roll Cooked cinnamon apples Milk	**12** Beef crunchy taco Cheese, lettuce Tomatoes Mexican rice Colorful corn Chips & salsa Milk	**13** Chicken pretzel Potatoes au gratin Fried okra Fruit medley Roll Milk	**14** Spaghetti w/ meat sauce Tossed salad Broccoli Garlic bread Ice cream sandwich Milk
17 Cheeseburger/Bun Baked beans Potato Chips Pineapple Rice Krispie Treat Milk	**18** Potato Skins w/ cheese & bacon Green beans Diced carrots Applesauce Roll Milk	**19** Salisbury Steak & gravy Creamed potatoes Corn Green peas Roll Milk	**20** Chicken on a bun Potato smiles Broccoli w/ cheese Dill pickles Orange wedge Milk	**21** **Teacher** **Work Day** **No School**
24 Popcorn Shrimp Macaroni & Cheese Green Peas Dill Pickles Roll Pineapple Milk	**25** Sloppy Joe on bun Corn Chips Green Beans Pears Chocolate chip cookie Milk	**26** Steak fingers Broccoli & Cheese Tater tots Mixed Fruit Roll Milk	**27** Chicken Sticks Rice & Gravy Baby Lima Beans Orange Wedges Roll Milk	**28** Cheese Pizza Carrots Green Salad Apples/Applesauce Chocolate Pudding Milk

Market conditions, delivery and availability of food may require changes in menus. Parents will be notified of any such changes

Back to School!

August 2003 **Back to School!**

Snack Menu

Monday	Tuesday	Wednesday	Thursday	Friday
4 Morning blueberry muffin orange juice Afternoon Cheez-its apple juice	**5** Morning Cheerios milk Afternoon cheese & saltines fruit punch juice	**6** Morning biscuit & grape jelly apple juice Afternoon Ritz crackers pineapple	**7** Morning bagel & cream cheese orange juice Afternoon sugar cookie green watermelon juice	**8** Morning fruit loops milk Afternoon Goldfish crackers peaches
11 Morning blueberry muffin orange juice Afternoon graham crackers apple juice	**12** Morning Cheerios milk Afternoon Ritz crackers blue raspberry juice	**13** Morning biscuit & grape jelly apple juice Afternoon Home Plate cookies white grape juice	**14** Morning bagel & cream cheese orange juice Afternoon animal crackers cherry juice	**15** Morning fruit loops milk Afternoon oranges vanilla wafers
18 Morning blueberry muffin orange juice Afternoon Cheez-its apple juice	**19** Morning Cheerios milk Afternoon cheese & saltines fruit punch juice	**20** Morning biscuit & grape jelly apple juice Afternoon Ritz crackers pineapple	**21** Morning bagel & cream cheese orange juice Afternoon sugar cookie green watermelon juice	**22** Morning fruit loops milk Afternoon Goldfish crackers peaches
25 Morning blueberry muffin orange juice Afternoon graham crackers apple juice	**26** Morning Cheerios milk Afternoon Ritz crackers blue raspberry juice	**27** Morning biscuit & grape jelly apple juice Afternoon Home Plate cookies white grape juice	**28** Morning bagel & cream cheese orange juice Afternoon animal crackers cherry juice	**29** Morning fruit loops milk Afternoon oranges vanilla wafers

Mar. 4. 2008 4:59PM   No. 1956   P. 2

September 2003

Lunch Menu

Monday	Tuesday	Wednesday	Thursday	Friday
1 Labor Day Center Closed	**2** Potato Skins w/ cheese & bacon Green beans Diced carrots Applesauce Roll Milk	**3** French toast sticks w/ syrup Sausage links Cheese slice Tater tots Peaches Milk	**4** Chicken on a bun French fries Broccoli w/ cheese Dill pickles Orange wedge Milk	**5** Pizza cheese sticks Marinara sauce Green beans Apples/Applesauce Chocolate ice cream cup Milk
8 Popcorn Shrimp Macaroni & Cheese Green Peas Dill Pickles Roll Pineapple Milk	**9** Sloppy Joe on bun Corn Chips Green Beans Pears Chocolate chip cookie Milk	**10** Steak fingers Broccoli & Cheese Tater tots Peaches Roll Milk	**11** Beef crunchy taco Cheese, lettuce Tomatoes Mexican rice Colorful corn Chips & salsa Milk	**12** Cheese pizza Carrots Green Salad Apples/Applesauce Ice cream sandwich Milk
15 Hamburger/bun French fries Peas & Carrots Peaches Vanilla ice cream cup Milk	**16** Beef Stew Yellow rice Apples/Applesauce Lima beans Cheesy Roll Milk	**17** Zesty ravioli Creamed corn Green beans Orange Wedge Garlic Bread Milk	**18** Chicken Nuggets Creamed potatoes Broccoli & cheese Roll Strawberry jell-o Milk	**19** Ham & Cheese Roll-up Corn chips Green beans Pineapple Wheat bread Brownie Milk
22 Tomato soup or Chicken noodle soup Grilled cheese sandwich Cooked carrots Peaches Oyster crackers Milk	**23** Sausage biscuit Cheese slice Hash brown Cooked cinnamon apples Milk	**24** Chicken nuggets Rice & gravy Baby limas Orange wedges Roll Milk	**25** Fish sticks Mashed potatoes Green beans Pears Roll Milk	**26** Cheese pizza Corn Green Salad Apple Wedges Chocolate ice cream cup Milk
29 Cheeseburger/Bun Baked beans Potato Chips Pineapple Rice Krispies Treat Milk	**30** Potato Skins w/ cheese & bacon Green beans Diced carrots Applesauce Roll Milk			

*Market conditions, delivery and availability of food may require changes in menus. Parents will be notified of any such changes

Church members are given the first opportunity for enrollment; the same is true for employing teachers and other service personnel. After that, kids from the community can enroll, provided they understand that part of the curriculum is a daily Bible lesson and a weekly chapel. All students are required to wear a uniform. There are no school busses so parents have to form carpools.

Susan reminds us that church schools must be certified by the local health department. Even if this is not mandatory it is highly recommended, and would include periodic inspections by the health department. This is a sensible policy from several standpoints.

Auxiliary Programs

Angel Food Ministries is dedicated to providing food and financial support to communities across the United States. It began in 1994 in the small Georgia town of Monroe when Pastors Joe and Linda Wingo were led to assist families in their area who had been affected by the closing of several industrial plants. What started there by serving 34 local families has now expanded to providing for persons in 35 states.

Each Angel Food box contains both fresh and frozen items with an average retail value of about $60. It will feed a family of four for about a week or a single senior for about a month at a cost of $30. This is the same high-quality food that one could purchase at a retail grocery store. No dented cans or out-of-date goods or overripe fruit are ever part of what this ministry provides. Angel has no qualifications, minimums, or income restrictions; everyone is encouraged to participate.

There are various host churches that collect the orders at the first of each month, and then later they will either pick food up from Angel's warehouse or have it delivered to them. Participants bring a large box with them to the site; it is packed by volunteers and the recipients leave with their order. Devotional materials are included in each food box. In April of 2008, each regular unit contained the following:

2 pounds fully-cooked meatloat
1 pound beef fajita strips
3 pounds breaded chicken
2 pounds ribs
2 pounds lasagna dinner
1 pound gourmet sausage
1 pound fully-cooked meatballs
16 ounces broccoli
15 ounces refried beans
12 tortillas
26 ounces pasta sauce
16 ounces pasta
6 ounces pancake mix
64 ounces chicken noodle soup
Fresh carrots, potatoes, and oranges, and at least one dessert item.

Those who have purchased a food box can opt for a monthly special at an additional cost of about $20, choosing from a variety grill box, a New York strip box, a stuffed chicken breast combo box, or a senior convenience meal box. The web site is angelfoodministries.com. 5

Must Ministries

Because people of God *must* serve others, this local ministry was founded in the metropolitan Atlanta area. It offers a "Loaves and Fishes" community kitchen, and relies upon corporate sponsors. They have fund raisers several times a year in order to provide canned goods and to help community members who ask for assistance. During winter months, Must offers emergency housing for women and children.

Must Ministries is particularly significant in times of escalating food prices and rising unemployment. Their website is mustministries.org. This ministry too is but one of thousands of similar programs across the United States.

Meditation: Jesus showed us a varied ministry, not always with adults, and not always with the successful. If we are to walk in His steps today, we must try to do the same. Thank you, God, for church members with the heart of a disciple, serving quietly and expecting nothing in return.

Chapter 4
Celebrations Unlimited

Psalm 100: "I was glad when they said unto me,
'Let us go into the house of the Lord'."

Banquets—You Want Us to Do What?

In Deuteronomy 14:22-27 we read God's instructions to the children of Israel about having a party. He tells them to set aside one-tenth of their wealth each year to be used to celebrate His presence among them. Everyone is to be invited, rich and poor, lame and blind, prostitutes, all the unsavory characters as well as the rabbis and village leaders. He wanted singing and dancing and everyone having a good time. Today, God still wants His people to have parties and enjoy themselves. He wants to meet our physical needs as well as our spiritual needs.

Most of the meals prepared and served at a church are regularly scheduled: Wednesday night supper, men's breakfasts, women's groups, administrative dinners, and a myriad of other program area meetings. With increasing frequency now food service is asked for a theme dinner, or a special banquet, or quite frankly, an outrageous event. Proverbs15:15 tells us that the cheerful heart has a continual feast, and those working in the church kitchen can certainly identify with the "continual."

One interesting event is at a church having a community Thanksgiving meal. Seeking something different from previous years, they began researching the pilgrims' story. And this is what they decided to do: they reasoned that nobody relocates from one place to another over the Thanksgiving holidays, and so they arranged with a moving company to have dinner served from their vans. That's right, it was dinner on the Mayflower! Ingenious, but not an easy thing to manage as there isn't lighting or electricity inside those vans. Most of the guests never even thought of this, and in a funny way this is a tribute to the wizards of church food service.

A popular banquet idea now is to get someone to host a table for 8 or 10 persons. There can be 10, 20, or 50 tables in the room. He or she may decorate the table in any way they wish, with any theme they choose, using dishes of their choice. The food is served on clear plastic plates (over the place setting) so the host may take their clean china and dirty silverware home with them to avoid confusion in the kitchen. Themes vary, some can be about ballet with napkins wrapped-and-tied like toe shoes, and then having a tutu as the centerpiece. Another favorite is a country theme with tin plates and agate cups. Washboards and old containers are in the center.

There can be a very formal and beautiful setting with candelabra, sterling silver, and fresh roses, or a favorite movie table featuring posters, theater tickets, and movie reels. Men like to have a golf table using fake grass as place mats with putting-green flags: teens can have rock n' roll as their theme; someone else wants to feature cars or classical music. The possibilities are endless, and the creativity of church members is amazing. This affords an opportunity of participation to persons who aren't comfortable teaching or visiting the sick. Thus food service ministers in its own unique way.

The fun part of the evening is when guests arrive and tour the room, examining each themed table. By the way, the table hosts are not identified. Guests are asked to pick their favorite in categories like "Most Original"; "Most Beautiful"; "Funniest," "Best Depiction of Theme"; "My Favorite," etc, the winners to be announced at the conclusion of the evening. This is a fun and effective fund-raiser, and members of the congregation love participating. If it seems that competition is not a good idea omit the awarding of prizes, and keep the dining area open for several days for paid "viewing," climaxing with a dinner on the last evening.

South Georgia is known for its plantations and quail hunts. Albany, Georgia is right in the middle of all this activity. Kaye Blalock, besides being Hospitality Director at First United Methodist, also owns a catering company called

Southern Elegance. We will read Kaye's remarks about her dual role in chapter five. The important thing about Kaye's philosophy is that "she dances with him who brung her." She keeps her focus on the church she serves and honors that commitment first.

It is not at all unusual for Kaye to serve 1,000 people for three days in a row during the height of quail season. Notable names and faces are guests for these events. Once when Kay was suffering with her leg while trying to serve the hunters, a well-known Army general came to her. "Sit down," he said. "Which leg is it and exactly where does it hurt?" Kaye showed him, and he clasped his hands around the spot, told her not to move, prayed for her relief, and when he released the leg, the pain was gone! A famous TV star asked for his dinner to be delivered to his room after recently having had major surgery. Kaye did it herself so she could meet him. Notable political persons come to quail hunts, and during one presidential administration Air Force II was often seen in the area.

Kaye uses the same servers over and over again. Each server is trained in one particular aspect of the meal, and will have this same function at every event. So, a salad person will always work on salads, desserts, only on desserts, and so on. One time for the Elks Lodge evening of travel they constructed a ship out of poster board, and then had destination rooms scattered about. There was a shuffleboard room, a casino, and an Hawaiian room for guests to visit. This event raised $20,000 for charity.

By the way, to build a volcano, get a piece of plywood. In the center using anchored chicken wire construct a volcano form. Roughly cover this with cement leaving a square hole at the top. Insert a halved milk carton. Fill with water and add dry ice to create a smoking effect. Caution: this is a heavy piece, so build it where you will use it.

To make palm trees alongside the volcano, up-end small three-legged stools. At your local grocery ask the produce clerk to save the outside of pineapples he opens to prepare pineapple chunks for sale. Encase the stool legs in these pineapple hulls with toothpicks, and they become the trunks of three palm trees. Top with a Boston fern, and your decoration is complete at very little expense.

At Roswell Presbyterian in Roswell, Georgia Molly Poister regularly hosts an event called Bachathon. It features guest organists in concert at the noon hour. For lunch Molly serves a "Bach Lunch." Also in Roswell, Pat Stamps created a chuck wagon, attaching wheels made out of poster board to an 8-foot table. By making arches over the table and draping them with a sheet, she created a Conestoga wagon for her barbecue dinner.

Based upon the popularity of the TV program, Teri Jones and crew at Hillside United Methodist in Woodstock, Georgia had an antiques roadshow evening. With the price of dinner a guest could have one item appraised by a local antiques dealer. The items were then displayed with their prices for all to see. They also did a dinner theater with the actors and actresses serving as waitpersons. After each act of the play, one part of the dinner was served: salad first, then soup, then entrée, then dessert, so guests ate a little, and watched a little of the performance before the next course.

"Hats Off To Spring" can be the theme of a brunch.

Everyone is given a Fred-Astaire-style straw hat, and an Easter basket contains the food. A sports event can require everyone to wear a uniform depicting their favorite sport, and a tailgate party can be held in the parking lot with guests serving their dishes from the back of their vehicle. This is also an effective way of having kids trick or treat in a safe environment.

Peachtree Road Methodist in Atlanta has a unique fashion show and boutique sale. Members are asked to donate designer or other colorful accessories and hats. A fashion show featuring some of the gowns highlights a dinner. Later all the donated items are offered for sale, first come, first served. Proceeds from the sale and the dinner are donated to a church project called "Mission Possible" which places homeless persons into a job and an apartment. Any unsold clothing is donated to the Atlanta Union Mission.

Wedding Receptions

This is the day the bride has waited for all her life. It is more than excellent food or a beautiful setting. This is the beginning of a new life and a new commitment. It is a threshold over which neither she nor the groom can ever pass again. Jesus blessed marriage by attending a wedding in Canna of Galilee, signaling that a couple should have the finest of everything for their reception.

This shrieks "important; do your very best" in the church kitchen. Without question there have never been any two wedding receptions exactly alike, so it is not possible to give a "fail safe" formula for one, but there are some things that work well in addition to the usual fare:

A chocolate station with bon bons, éclairs, a chocolate fountain, rich brownies, and mousse in tart shells.

A cheese station featuring a queso dip, a board with exotic cheeses, and a molded spread covered with strawberry jam.

Spiced pecans and almonds to munch on.

Carving stations featuring beef, turkey, or ham.

A pasta station with several pastas and several sauces.

A fresh strawberry tree with berries affixed to a styrofoam cone.

Memorial Receptions

With more frequency than ever before churches are hosting memorial services that are followed by a reception. This is a real trend in the past 5 years. Several reasons come to mind. In large cities many of the funeral homes are now part of a consortium, and as a result, the personal touch that is so necessary at this time may be missing. The bereaved turn to their church for solace and for comfort. In the valley of the shadow of death, they are comforted by the sanctuary of their church home.

Another part of this changing trend is the increasing number of memorial services as compared to funerals. Adding to this number is a private family interment followed by a memorial service, sometimes not even on the same day. The number of cremations is also on the increase. Thus, lacking the urgency to go to the cemetery, families can spend time after a service visiting with friends in a setting better equipped to handle a crowd than their home. A final reason is financial in that generally there is no charge beyond food for the service at the church whereas there will be significant charges at the funeral home.

In these instances the receptions are generally low key with punch and cookies only being served.

Hints and Timesavers

Make a mock hollandaise sauce by combining one can (any size) of cream of chicken soup, ½ can of mayonnaise, and then adding fresh lemon juice and mustard to taste. Grated cheese and curry powder may be added to make a sauce for chicken divan. It also is very good for eggs benedict or steamed asparagus.

For a quick dessert put 1 #10 can of pie filling into a hotel pan. If using a commercial size, cover with 1/3 box (would be 2 boxes from the grocery store) of dry yellow cake mix. Dot with butter. Bake at 350 degrees until the cake mix is browned. Chopped nuts may also be added to the topping.

An excellent dessert is a prepared product called chocolate cobbler. Sysco food service carries this product.

Save those rinds you cut off cheeses. Store in the freezer, and drop into soups or stews for extra flavor and thickening.

For a better barbecue sauce cut a bottled sauce by ½ to $^1/_3$ with salsa, mild or hot to your taste.

If your soup or stew is too thin to suit, add small amounts of instant mashed potato granules until you are satisfied with the consistency.

Two useful websites are cooksrecipes.com, and epicurious.com.

Tired of the mess when serving a tossed salad on the same plate as the rest of the meal? Use squat glasses for the salad. Put two small romaine leaves vertically at the back of the glass. Fill with dressed tossed salad for each guest and garnish with grape tomatoes. Easier to serve and easier to eat.

Try adding peach pie filling to a fresh fruit salad. It binds the fruit together, and keeps it from turning brown. No one will realize what the secret ingredient is.

For a very easy fruit salad freeze #303 cans of fruit cocktail. After they are frozen, remove both ends of the can, slide the frozen fruit cocktail out, slice, and serve on a bed of lettuce. Garnish with a dressing of vanilla yogurt mixed with some lemonade concentrate and a bit of almond flavoring.

Purchase day-old doughnuts and use them as the basis of bread pudding. Using fruit-filled ones makes it especially yummy.

Try substituting flavored coffee creamer for milk in dessert recipes.

Recipes

Blueberry Salad
(serves 10)

2 small packages cranberry Jello
2 c hot water
1 can blueberry pie filling
16 oz sour cream
8 oz cream cheese

Mix Jello and hot water until dissolved. When it begins to thicken, add pie filling and chill until set (it might be useful to add a package of plain gelatin to insure a firm set). Mix sour cream, cream cheese, and powdered sugar and spread on top of Jello. To vary, add drained, crushed pineapple, or toasted pecans, or substitute peach or cherry pie filling and select a different flavor Jello.

Roast Beef Salad
(serves 50)

25 c cooked roast beef
6 c French dressing
3 c chopped pickles
6 ½ c mayonnaise
25 c dices cooked potatoes
6 c coarsely grated carrot
24 hard cooked eggs, chopped

Marinate beef in French dressing for 2 hours. Combine with all other ingredients. Serve on lettuce leaf.

Frosted Grapes
(serves 150)

24 lbs grapes, washed and picked from stem
1 (commercial size) box brown sugar
6 lbs sour cream
3 ½ c rum flavoring

Mix all the above and refrigerate overnight. Remix and then serve.

Texas Caviar

(contributed by Teri Sawyer, First Baptist, Tyler)
Serves 30 or more.

3 cans black-eyed peas, rinsed and drained
3 cans yellow corn, drained
1 can tomatoes with chilies
½ large purple onion, finely chapped
1 each red, yellow, and green bell pepper, finely chopped
4 T cilantro, chopped
1/3 c olive oil
1/3 c fresh lime juice
½ t salt
½ t chili powder
½ t cayenne pepper
¼ c sugar

Combine ingredients down to the olive oil in a large bowl.
Combine remaining ingredients in a separate bowl, mix and
pour over vegetables. Cover tightly and refrigerate at least 8
hours. Toss several times during this period. Taste and add
seasonings you prefer. Can be served as an hors d' oeuvre
with tortilla chips, or as a salad. More servings if used as an
hors d' oeuvre.

Heavenly Potatoes

(serves 50) from Sandy Smathers, Crabapple First Baptist, Alpharetta, Georgia

10 lb fresh hash brown potatoes
3 lb sour cream
50 oz cream of chicken soup, undiluted
2 ½ lb shredded sharp cheddar cheese
2 c chopped onion
2# nacho chips,crushed
1 c melted margarine

Combine all ingredients except chips and margarine. Mix well. Pour into well-greased hotel pans, covering with chips and drizzling with margarine. Bake at 350 degrees until bubbly, about 25 minutes.

Spinach a la Garner
(serves 50)

140 oz frozen chopped spinach
1# diced onion
3 1/2 c. melted margarine
2 t. seasoned salt
14 eggs, beaten
3 ½ c grated Parmesan cheese
2 T garlic powder
1 t. thyme

Cook and drain spinach well. Blend remaining ingredients and add to spinach. Put into prepared hotel pans and bake 40-50 minutes until set.

Corn Pudding
(50 servings)

3 c sugar
1 doz. eggs
78 oz evaporated milk
1 ½ c. cornstarch
96 oz cream style corn
36 oz niblet corn
¾ c margarine

Combine sugar and cornstarch. Add beaten eggs, two kinds of corn, and evaporated milk. Mix well. Pour into prepared hotel pans. Dot top with margarine. Bake 1 hour at 350 degrees, or until center is almost firm.

Very Easy Quiche
(for each pie)

1 unbaked 9" pie shell
½ lb ground beef or sausage or chicken (may omit meat and use chopped spinach or mushrooms)
½ c mayonnaise
½ c milk
2 eggs, well beaten
½ cup sliced spring onion
1 ½ c cheese, grated (Swiss, gruyere, white or yellow cheddar is best).

Cook meat, if needed. If using frozen spinach make sure it is completely thawed and patted dry. Mix remaining ingredients and pour into pie shell. Bake at 350 degrees for 35 minutes until knife inserted in center comes out clean.

Angel Chicken Pasta

(serves 35) from Sandy Smathers, Crabapple First Baptist, Alpharetta, Georgia

35 skinless boneless chicken breast halves
1 1/3 c butter
1 large envelope dry Italian-style dressing mix
3 c white wine or chicken broth
51 oz cream of mushroom soup, undiluted
1 ½ # cream cheese
angel hair pasta for 35

Melt butter over low heat, stir in dressing mix. Blend wine and soup and stir in. Mix in softened cream cheese and stir until smooth. Heat through, being careful not to boil. Arrange chicken breasts in a single layer in a hotel pan, covering with sauce. Bake, uncovered 35-45 minutes at 350 degrees. While this is in the oven, cook pasta al dente.

Serve chicken and sauce over pasta.

Seafood Casserole
(serves 40)

10 c stuffing mix
5 # seafood (crab, baby shrimp or a mixture of both)
5 c mayonnaise
½ c fresh lemon juice
10 c milk
5 c chopped celery (or green or red pepper or both)
1 ¼ c chopped onion
2 T Worcestershire sauce

Pour milk over stuffing mix and allow to sit until the stuffing has softened. Mix remaining ingredients and stir into stuffing. Pour into prepared pan and bake at 350 degrees 35-45 minutes or until browned.

Susan's Beef Brisket

(contributed by Susan McElwain, First United Methodist, Marietta, Georgia)

1 7-8# beef brisket
1 pkg onion soup mix
2 onions, sliced
1 T garlic powder
1 c ketchup

Sauce: 1 bottle chili sauce; 1 8 oz jar apricot preserves, 1 #303 can sauerkraut, not drained.

Combine soup mix, garlic powder, and ketchup. Rub into brisket and place in a roasting pan. Put sliced onions on top. Add water to the pan, just a small amount (do not cover meat). Cover and bake at 325 degrees for 3 hours. Let cool, scrape the onions and sauce off the meat and save. Slice the meat against the grain and return to the pan. Add reserved onions and sauce. Mix the last three ingredients and put on top of sliced meat. Allow to marinate for several days. Reheat at 325 degrees for 1 hour and serve. Serves 16 to 20 people.

Santa Fe Chicken Soup
(serves 32)

4 T butter
2 c chopped spring onions
2 gal chicken broth
12 c chopped cooked chicken
1 #10 can pinto beans, rinsed and drained
12 oz chopped green chillies, drained

Saute the onion in butter. Add other ingredients, bring to a boil, reduce heat and simmer 30 minutes to an hour. Garnish with baked tortilla strips and a little chopped cilantro.

Mincemeat Pound Cake
(serves 100)

2 2/3 c shortening
Scant 4T baking soda
1 gal flour
3 ½ qt canned mincemeat
1 ½ qt brown sugar
1 2/3 T salt
2 c water

Cream together shortening, brown sugar, baking soda, and salt in mixer at medium speed about 4 minutes. Add flour and water alternately, blending well after each addition. Add mincemeat while blending at low speed, but do not overmix. Pour 2 qts matter into each of 4 prepared loaf pans. Bake 1 ½ hours at 325 degrees. Cool. Cut into 25 slices per loaf.

English Toffee Crunch Cake
(serves 80)

Prepare 1 2lb.4 oz white cake mix as directed on box, adding 1 ¼ c vegetable oil and 12 eggs. Cool completely and refrigerate. For frosting, beat 8 c heavy whipping cream with 1 t instant coffee until stiff peaks form. Add 6 c coarsely chopped English toffee candy bars and frost cake. Serve immediately or refrigerate.

Amish-Style Cookies

(makes 150)
contributed by Teri Sawyer, First Baptist, Tyler, Texas

1 c white granulated sugar
1 c powdered sugar
1 c butter, softened
1 c cooking oil
2 large eggs
4 ½ c flour
1 t baking soda
1 t cream of tartar
1 t vanilla, lemon, or almond extract

Cream together first 4 ingredients. Add remaining ingredients, mixing well. Drop small balls onto greased cookie sheet; flatten slightly with a fork. Bake at 375 degrees for 10 to 12 minutes.

Lemon Curd

(contributed by Susan McElwain, Marietta First United
Methodist, Marietta, Georgia)

1 c sugar
½ c butter
zest and strained juice of 3 lemons
3 eggs, beaten well

Put all ingredients in a heavy saucepan. Cook over low heat
stirring constantly until mixture thickens, but still falls easily
from a spoon. Do not boil.

Refrigerate or freeze. Use as a topping on cake or as a filling
for tarts.

Meditation: Jesus chose unusual settings in which to teach. Mountainsides, the Sea of Galilee, and public streets all were venues. Not everyone, then or now, is reached in the same manner or by the same thing. We want our member or guest to be glad when someone says to them, "Let us go into the house of the Lord." Today's churches have different unusual settings, but the "unusualness" remains an essential part of reaching out to all people.

Members of the National Association of Church Food Service have adopted this statement of purpose:

"We believe that food service is an equal ministry of the church, touching the congregation as no other department can. We believe our trust in God affirms our work and empowers us to do His will."

"We feel our role is to provide the opportunity for fellowship in a loving atmosphere, and we have a commitment to ourselves and the church we serve."

"We believe excellence in our work is a part of this commitment, and pledge ourselves to this goal."

Amen.

Chapter 5
The Red Sea Closes In

Proverbs 5:14 "I have come to the brink
of utter ruin in the midst of the whole assembly."

The Setting

The church kitchen is a unique venue. It is not true that what works in the usual commercial kitchen will work well at a church. Church food service, unlike any other, is program driven, meaning that if the staff doesn't plan events, the kitchen may lie idle, and if they plan a lot, it becomes a stressful work environment. People go to restaurants to eat, but at a church people normally eat as part of a larger experience. In other words, the meal is not usually the main reason they are present. Thus, kitchen planners operating in their normal mode can miss some important details.

For instance, a restaurant may serve 300 people between 6pm and 10pm. It can easily have dishes and glassware and silver for only 150, because it can wash and reuse these items in the same evening. Church food service may also serve 300 persons in an evening, but they do it between 6pm and 6:10pm rather than over a three or four-hour time frame. Thus a church kitchen needs full dish service for the maximum number of persons who will ever be served, but rapid recovery of these items is not critical. This affects warewashing equipment and storage.

To further complicate matters, each church is different and has different food service needs. We see that some have grade schools, almost all have preschools or daycare, and there are additional programs like meals-on-wheels, soup kitchens, multiple banquets, community events, and seasonal programs for their own congregation. Each one of these intended uses impacts the equipment chosen and how it fits into the available space.

A restaurant is a restaurant is a restaurant. They may move some tables around for a wedding reception, but generally their format and set-up remain constant. Their cuisine is what is on the menu, and their décor constant. Their equipment is purchased to accommodate their specific menu. They do not need to produce a variety of dishes with various themes and presentations. A Chinese restaurant does not need stations and staff to produce a large array of salads.

A church fellowship hall on the other hand may be the site of a banquet for 400, a wedding reception, a Jerusalem marketplace, and a pancake breakfast all in one weekend.

Each planning group comes with their own particular needs and wants. If linens are to be used they must coordinate with the theme of the event, and décor varies from casual to elegant, also matching the theme. The only thing that is constant is change.

Method of Service

Method of service greatly impacts kitchen design. There are basically only two methods of getting food to the diner: take it to them, or they come and get it. There are variations on these of course, but they don't change the basic method. Salads can be preset before a banquet, eaten first, and then the guest goes to the buffet line for the main course. Same with desserts or beverages. The plated meal requires service personnel who are trained to refill water glasses, bring another knife or more butter, and in general pay more attention to the guest. Needless to say, table service is the most expensive option because of the additional personnel required, and because such personnel are not interchangeable with employees who prepare the food. Asking the assistant cook to go and do table service does not work.

Often churches must be prepared for both methods of service. This is not true of school lunch rooms, of hospitals, or of restaurants except on rare occasions. If table service is an option, then plate covers and holding cabinets are useful, but necessary is plating space in what may already be a crowded kitchen. If buffet service is primary, then equipment that makes this possible is at the top of the list. Nothing can torpedo a nice meal faster than a pot straight from the stove with a long-handled spoon in it on the buffet table. These items are great for cooking, but really poor for presentation. It is incredibly important that serving pieces placed on a buffet line are attractive, serviceable, and clean. That seems obvious, doesn't it? Clean. After a while on the buffet line utensils can be rust-stained, lose their shine, or become bent. These items represent a minor expense and should be discarded before their appearance telegraphs the wrong message about food service.

If there are volunteers working behind steam tables this calls for yet another type of equipment, much of which is a permanent installation. Buffet tables can be moved or removed to other locations, but steam tables are a fixture because they require heavy-duty electricity, and occasionally, plumbing as well. The point in all of this is that purchasing equipment can be disastrous without thorough knowledge of how food will get from the kitchen to the customer's plate. Lots of unused equipment sits in the corners of fellowship halls with plastic flowers, testimony to lack of advance planning.

Where Are the Green Beans?

Among other pre-planning failures is lack of appropriate storage space. It takes a lot of readily-accessible storage to enable rapid transition from one event to another. Even the most loyal staff member or volunteer will balk at going to the basement to get table decorations, and it is pretty certain that no one will take them back when the event is over. There have been instances where used candles and decorations were found heaped on the back of a stage ten years after their usage! Many stages hold old treasures that have become time capsules of that church's activities. This is not a good advertisement of the church's stewardship.

There are church kitchens that have so little planned storage that unopened cases of food sit in a corner stacked on top of each other. Oh, where are the green beans? Didn't we order them? Complicating this situation is that vendors have what is called a "minimum order," which is a threshold number of cases of food to be delivered or a minimum dollar amount of the invoice. Thus daily delivery of a small number of items is not possible. In some of the smaller cities, deliveries only are made to their area once or twice weekly. Sometimes this means the food service director has to go by the grocery store or large warehouse every time a meal is to be prepared. Not only is this time consuming, it also is a very expensive way to purchase food.

As we have observed, church food service changes its theme and method of service from week to week. To pull this off smoothly, many items are needed, and more importantly, they must be stored conveniently. One church learned this lesson the hard way. It was decided to have permanent floral arrangements on the tables so they would look nice all the time. A great idea that lasted two days until the next program area wanted them removed, but there was no place to put them. They too were assigned to that stage.

Moved back and forth, dropped and handled, they were soon discarded. Better no decorations at all than shabby ones; maybe these could have been saved if whether or not to have them or where-to-keep-them had been decided before they were purchased.

Matthew tells us in Chapter 7:24-27 about building our house on a firm foundation. He says that a wise man builds his house on a rock, and that rains and wind beat upon it, yet it does not fall. The foolish man builds his house on sand, and when the rains come and the winds blow, it will fall with a great crash.

Mission Accomplished...or Was It?

With all this knowledge we can now witness the result of some "great ideas":

One well-meaning architect designed a kitchen with two T-shaped serving areas. The base of each "T" served as the waiting line with the top of the "T" being the actual food service area. There were two serving lines at the top of each "T," so that as guests entered they could choose to go either right or left to get their dinner. Volunteers were to serve the plates as each person passed by.

The new open kitchen was located immediately behind the two serving lines. It was estimated that this arrangement would enable serving 400 people (100 at each of the 4 lines) in 15 minutes. Easy access from the kitchen to the service areas was thought to be a major advantage, as well as the ability to selectively close lines as needed. Sounds pretty good, right? This is what actually happened, though.

In order to serve the plates each food line needed 4 volunteers, a total of 16 for every large meal. "Let the dinner begin!" And it did, smoothly at first. Shortly, kitchen personnel heard shouts of, "We're out of potatoes!" and they raced to line 1, then line 2, trying to figure out who it was that needed potatoes. On their journey, they learned that line 3 was out of rolls. It was basically mass confusion compounded by the fact that there was a tile partition separating the two main "T" lines. Thus there was neither visual nor oral communication. Neither side could see how many people were waiting to be served so that they could transition food from one line to another. Therefore line 4 with 8 people waiting in line to be served got an entire pan (32 servings) of meatloaf while there was no meatloaf for line 2 with 20 people waiting.

The worst part—yet another 20/20 hindsight revelation- was that the 16 volunteers arrived in the kitchen seeking aprons and instruction just shortly before the dinner was to begin. There were different volunteers every week, and their arrival came at the crunch time in food preparation, interfering with its completion. Of course it was vital that the volunteers know their assignment like how much corn is a serving and whether or not someone can skip the vegetable and have two servings of the starch, but a training session before the actual event would have helped enormously. It is well to consider that someone had to recruit the volunteers, schedule kitchen personnel, and try to replace absentees.

Human nature plays a mighty role in this too, if servers favor their friends and clergy with extra portions. Service will be slowed if there are private conversations in the food line. None of this is awful in and of itself, but both are considerations when planning large dinners. It is also well to avoid having two best friends side-by-side and having all the slow servers on the same line. Earlier, a most important side of this called hospitality was addressed.

The Scullery

Another trend in food service design that has worked its way into churches is having a scullery. A scullery is a separate dishwashing and storage area where all those dirty dishes and the noise they create can be isolated. Super in the dining room, but are you getting an image here of Cinderella? The guest places used dishes on a state-of-the-art conveyor belt which magically whisks them away. Meanwhile, in the scullery, a lone attendant wrestles with removing the dishes before they crash, sort of like the Lucy Ricardo/Ethel Mertz experience at the candy factory. Teetering stacks of dirty plates, not all the same size, and used glasses all of which need to be emptied and racked for washing accumulate on the scullery floor. This is workable where there are multiple attendants at the conveyor belt, but churches just do not usually have the funds to supply these extra personnel. The physical atmosphere in a scullery can be overwhelming as steam from the dish machine blends with dirty dinner dishes.

Designing a Church Kitchen

Bottom line is that the most important part of planning or redesigning a church kitchen is knowing what is expected before pouring cement or ordering equipment. The best source of this information is the food service director who can evaluate the plans so that the end result is the one desired. Complications arise when someone's notion becomes a part of building plans without careful evaluation by a knowledgeable church food service coordinator. The best "expert" is the person who has been or will be working in the new environment. Amazingly, lots of new kitchens are built without the workers ever seeing the plans, or seeing them only after someone else (who has no practical experience) has approved them.

Employees

We believe that people who work at a church have been "called" to do so, and in most cases this is true. A possible exception is the kitchen staff who can be hourly employees working for minimum wage. They may not have been called except by telephone. Lacking much training or education they are just trying to earn a living. They may not see working at the church as any different from working at a fast-food place.

And so their toleration of work and work conditions is limited whereas staff members in other church departments tend to be forgiving. At that fast food place there are shifts which protect the employees from extended work hours. Shift work is not the format of most churches. Expecting these workers to continually go the extra mile because they work for the church is probably not realistic.

Another part of the threatening sea can be having a kitchen staff that just cannot do the job. Sometimes the work and the worker do not match, and the green beans are mushy and tasteless. This is not satisfying for either the director or the staff, and if a serious talk does not rectify the problem then it is time to make a change. Hanging on with a person and hoping to see improvement is not a good long-term option. Terminating an employee is not going to be any easier in 6 weeks or 6 months than it is today if it needs doing.

Catering from the Kitchen

Some churches have decided that a good way to employ a quality food service director is to grant him/her the ability to use the church kitchen and equipment to cater their own private events off campus. Lots of times this turns out to be a good arrangement. The church gets a person whom they could not afford to employ otherwise; the food service director has space and equipment not possible otherwise. Kaye Blalock of First United Methodist Church in Albany, Georgia has this arrangement, and both Kaye and the church benefit from it. Kaye's philosophy is the root of her success. She says, "The church always comes first!" And she proves this by using her silver for church functions, and offering Southern Elegance menus to church events that could not afford it otherwise. She never turns down a church event because of a Southern Elegance party.

There can be drawbacks, though. Regardless of any hold harmless agreement signed between the caterer and the church, if someone gets sick eating the caterer's food, the church will be sued. The person suing may not win, but it can be a major hassle and a good-sized expense for the church to defend it. Therefore it is a good idea to require the caterer to maintain a liability policy of at least $1,000,000.

Then there is the question of food service employees. Whose event are they working on, anyway? And that aluminum foil and butter, whose is that? Volunteers are called in to help, but they could be enabling paid employees to work on one of the caterer's events. It is all a matter of both parties being fully aware of the circumstances, including the use of employees and the cost of the aluminum foil. The church may be willing to cover these expenses, but they often are not even aware of them. Another good idea would be to establish a caterer-use-of-kitchen fee that would apply to the church caterer as well as to any others using the facility.

An excellent caterer can attract people to the church. They attend a reception, think it's really good, and then visit the church and become involved. The opposite is true also. So in making this kind of arrangement with the food service director it is well to remember that their outside events reflect strongly on the church where they work. Good or bad, it will be the church that is perceived as responsible. It is also wise for the church to be aware of the number of private events being catered from its kitchen in order to maintain a proper balance between personal and church events. Kaye's philosophy that the church always comes first should be the guiding principle.

Meditation: If a terrible financial plague has descended upon a food service operation, and if all hearts have been hardened, remember what Moses said to the Hebrews as they were about to cross the Red Sea, "Stand firm and you will see.... deliverance. The Lord will fight for you" (Exodus 14:13). God caused the wheels of the Egyptian chariots to come off, stranding them as the sea closed in.

We may not find ourselves chased by an army but we nonetheless can feel trapped. God can intervene for us in any situation.

Chapter 6
How Firm Is Your Foundation?

*Isaiah 28:16 "See, I lay a stone in Zion, a tested stone,
a precious cornerstone for a sure foundation."*

There is a Biblical verse that is often misquoted as "Money is the root of all evil; in fact the actual words Paul wrote are, "For the love of money is the root of all evil (I Timothy 6:10). So we are not instructed to think of money as a bad thing; we are instructed to think carefully about its uses and about our involvement with it. When we are thoughtful with money we are being good stewards, and when we are not, we are being wasteful. Money is the elephant in the room, be it a corporation, a small business, a family, or a church.

A past governor of the state of Georgia was once asked what he thought was needed to relieve the state's beleaguered prison system. "Very simple," he said, "just send me a better class of criminal." Similarly, the way to hold down the cost of operating the church kitchen is to have no weekend work, rotate among only three or four menus, and charge the going market rate for meals. Simple.

The vibrant and dynamic churches of the twenty-first century would strike out on all these, because church food service today is an intricate and constantly-changing operation. A large number function under a blurry financial structure. In one way or another every church subsidizes their food service operation. This includes hidden costs such as the building, insurance, electricity, and natural gas, all of which are part of the larger church budget. These items are not just provided for the kitchen but for all other departments as well.

It is puzzling to understand why expectations of the kitchen's financial performance seem to be different from the other departments. Every one of them is totally subsidized; yet that subsidy is called budget. This is important to understand: the kitchen is certainly not the only department to collect money for a service, but it is usually the only department to be set out as having a subsidy. We don't think of education, music, or worship as "going in the hole." Only the kitchen has this distinction. So it starts off under a financial cloud.

Let's examine expectations first. What financial performance the church wishes of its food service department is very important to define. Widely touted is the old "break-even" theory, but that is a poor standard to use. If the kitchen does not break even it is by definition operating in the red, and finance committees all over the country will be horrified. Much better is to set the standard higher and aim for profit. Gasp! Money changers in the Temple!

Profit is thought of as a no-no and is thus considered an unacceptable option, but it really shouldn't be. Read I Corinthians 16:1-3. In these verses Paul says that we should set aside a sum of money each week, saving it up, so that no collections will have to be made when he arrives. Thus, when a church kitchen operates at a profit and saves that surplus, it allows that kitchen to provide for equipment repair and replacement, and enhancements like beautiful trays and punch bowls. There is also a cushion to cover any unforeseen expenses, none of which would come from tithes and offerings.

A moment here about food purchases. Probably there are as many new and innovative products available in the food service industry today as there are in any industry. Preprepared desserts are available. Main dishes such as roast beef can be purchased precooked to your order. Many tasty premade salads, frozen soups, and vegetables are on the market. Purchasing these items sometimes is not only desirable, but also advisable. By taking advantage of these things, a limited kitchen staff can produce quality back-to-back meals. Preprepared items may also enable your members to enjoy entrée items that are beyond staff skills. Occasional use can freshen a menu cycle.

Beware of using convenience items too frequently, for they are costly. For instance, 64 servings of ready-to-serve New York cheesecake would cost about $2.75 per serving.

Making cheesecake from a mix would cost less than $1.00 per serving. Regularly serving expensive desserts and entrees will wreck food cost.

A good way to prevent financial difficulties is for the finance committee and the food service director to make a list of all expected expenses and then designate who is responsible for paying for them. Included in the list should be groceries, paper goods, supplies, decorations, repair/replacement of equipment, new china and silver, labor and overtime wages, laundry and uniform, and salaries. Neither party to the agreement spends money that is not within their list of responsibilities without consulting the other. This is a one-time only procedure; once the ground rules have been established it will only be necessary to make occasional refinements.

Paul describes to us in I Timothy 1:1-13 the standards to be an overseer (i.e. pastor, leader, or other person of authority). He is to have a good reputation, be above reproach, sincere, and worthy of respect. How else will he be able take care of God's church? Paul says that being an overseer is a noble task. This doesn't just refer to the more-visible on the church staff or in the congregation.

Rule 1: The church must determine what specific costs it is willing to assume and what costs the food service operation must recover.

What's Yours, Mine, or Ours?

There should be a clear understanding that leads to agreement with the food service director that the church's goals are attainable without undue pressure on the kitchen or a loss in the quality of the food served. Then the food service manager who has agreed to these conditions must perform according to the standards that were mutually set. Criticizing the director after there is a financial crisis is not helpful for anyone. It can quickly become a venting session.

This is when the "shoulds" come out, dreadful creatures with chicken-bone horns and broccoli heads. They know everything about what should have been done, and want to dwell on that instead of making corrections for the future. Ban the "shoulds"; their mission is neither positive nor helpful.

Ecclesiastes 1:15 says nicely to let what is past be past: "What is twisted cannot be straightened; what is lacking cannot be counted." A slip-up when discovered and corrected can actually be positive, if at the next accounting it is neither twisted nor lacking. If it remains in that state however, it is time to take corrective action.

Rule 2: Meal prices are best set by experts in food service.

It Ain't Cheap and It Sure Ain't Easy

Whoowee! This can be a slippery slide into the canyon of no return. Clergy and staff want people to come to events at the church, and they think that low lunch and dinner prices will help to insure success. Perhaps this is true. This can become a sticky political issue. They may say that this is what the subsidy is for, but there is no subsidy that will consistently overcome insufficient meal prices. It will never work to position food service between the expectations of the church and the inability to set meal prices which would enable those expectations.

The food service director is the expert about what price is realistic, but shouldn't be alone in setting meal rates. A good way to spread the responsibility around is to use the finance committee as the authority to set meal prices. They would be set across the board after conferring with the director and staff; all lunches a certain price; all dinners a certain price. The director can negotiate upwards based upon the menu or method of service, but no one can go below the set rate because they're only having spaghetti. Having a smorgasbord of meal prices actually allows the customer to barter prices which will shortly come back to haunt the food service director. Having set meal rates willkeep food service healthy financially; the profit from an inexpensive meal offsets the deficit on an expensive one. In this way everyone benefits eventually.

Choosing between bad and good isn't really hard; what is hard is choosing between good and good. The food service director often is asked to make this judgment. The group that is coming has no budget; they work for underprivileged persons, and they are trying to keep the cost of this event low so they have more to give to their charity. This is true of 95% of persons who seek food service from a church. If the director tries to decide which group is more deserving of a discount than another, that director will perish in the mashed potato walls of the canyon. "Sorry, I can't negotiate prices because they are set by the finance committee. You are free to contact them if you wish." This is a powerful support and takes responsibility off the lone shoulders of the food service director. It is also the financially responsible way to act.

Something that can help with the financial health of the kitchen is to book outside groups, and charge them more than the same meal would cost at a church event. Same food cost plus higher revenue equals more profit. Once again, get the authorization of the finance committee to charge this higher rate. An aside is that this outside group may be charged a room rental fee in addition to the meal. This helps offset the expense in the maintenance department for set up and clean up, and would be credited to Building rather than Food Service. This type scheduling is good for the church as well as the outside group whose only other option is a hotel. The church will be an incredible bargain for them.

Rule 3: Requiring monthly performance reports is a good idea.

I Don't Do Numbers; I Do Food

Even with a good system set in place problems can arise and go undetected. So it is to everyone's advantage that food service submit a monthly report to a designated individual probably in the finance office. The sound like a tornado we're hearing now is the cumulative sigh from kitchens all over the country. Managers are already heavily burdened with details, and unlike other departments in the church, most do not have an administrative assistant to handle them or take their telephone messages. Remember that many workers in the kitchen lack formal education. So in addition to menu planning, cooking, ordering from vendors, handling inventory and storage, maybe clearing tables or washing dishes, now they need to be accountants as well.

Yep, this is true. If the food service director does not manage his operation then somebody else somewhere in the church will. It could be a volunteer, or the choir director, or a church secretary who assumes this role. Better to work that extra hour and know what is going on financially than to be informed later of problems by the "shoulds."

A large part of financial health is food costing every meal. Even kitchen experts can't correctly and consistently estimate the dollar value of all foods used in a meal. Although setting up the system was cumbersome in the past, computers and computer programs of the present make this job simpler and easier to manage. Seeing the bottom-line figures on each meal enables the manager to pinpoint loss leaders as well as profit makers. There are many software programs that will help with this; two of them are Micros and ChefTec.

Similarly, the finance office should provide food service with their version of financial performance at the end of each month. Details of what information is contained in both reports needs to be worked out jointly. It isn't necessary to have lengthy or burdensome details from either side, but joint agreement on current status is of unbelievable help, a roadmap out of the canyon. So often what we think happened isn't what happened at all.

Rule 4: The road to success is blocked by "free" food and beverage.

Have a Cup of Coffee, the Church Pays for It

Coffee, coffee everywhere and how the cents do shrink; free coffee, coffee everywhere, not if we were to think. Didja ever wonder how the disciples saved one soul without a cup of coffee in their hands? Or chicken in a pocket?

Nothing in food service is "free." There is a cost to every morsel and every drop. Somebody somewhere is paying, and it usually is food service. The question isn't whether or not it is a good idea to have lots of coffee available for members, of course it is. The question is "who foots the bill?" This can be an unrecognized expense, and it can be significant.

As a practical matter there is no satisfactory way to charge a member for a single cup of coffee; however this doesn't mean that the kitchen should furnish it gratis. A good bit of coffee is consumed on Sunday, so perhaps each Sunday school class could make a donation once a year to offset the cost. It goes without saying that the donation should reflect fair market rates. It doesn't normally work to have a basket with a note saying ."50 cents per cup," but it might work one Wednesday evening to take a coffee love offering. Or the church can designate part of their subsidy for coffee. This also applies to lemonade, hot chocolate, punch, tea, and certainly bottled water that are served, but not as an accompaniment to a meal. It isn't the replacement of the freezer that sends food service into a downward spiral, it is the steady leakage of undetected money.

Today with a Starbucks around every corner the church member wants a latte, or a hazelnut-flavored brew or other exotic blend, regular and decaf. Some churches are actually installing coffee bars with 4 kinds of sugar, 4 kinds of creamer, whipped cream, and chocolate shavings. That significant expense has now become huge. The idea of special coffees is a good one if the expense incurred is planned for.

There is a company that specializes in designing coffee bars for book stores. They will tell you that coffee bars are not profit centers; instead they act as a drawing card for shoppers. It is very welcoming for a church to have tables with members meeting there for coffee. Consider this an ambience that may attract, but do not expect it to provide an income stream. The company is Design Identity for more information.

And now, how about free meals for staff and clergy? They

have a committee meeting after the Wednesday supper and are forced to stay after work, and so should they have to pay for their dinner under these circumstances? Probably not. But should food service be expected to underwrite this expense? Probably not. Staff and clergy have budgets they can use to pay for their food, and this is an appropriate expense for them. They will recognize this if it is pointed out.

A subsidy that the kitchen provides the church is the family rate. You know what this is, a limit on the amount any family regardless of size pays for regularly-scheduled church meals. Just for illustration purposes let us say that the adult meal rate is $5.00, and the child's rate (which is in itself a subsidy) is $3.00. They would pay $19.00 to eat if they have three children. At a family rate of $15.00, there is a $4.00 difference that is expected to be absorbed by the kitchen if anybody thinks about it. It is probably a good idea to mention this casually in a finance committee meeting, and perhaps to give a yearly brief report on food service that mentions these subsidies.

The same logic applies to senior rates and all other discounted meals. When the food service director orders from vendors, there is no discount because "this chicken is for senior citizens"; nor is that chicken cheaper to cook or serve. This is not to quarrel with the policy of making some meals more affordable. This may be the correct thing to do. This is to bring an awareness of it, and highlight a contribution made by food service that may otherwise go unrecognized.

Rule 5: Having a food service committee can be an incredible help.

Oh, No, Not Another Committee!

The makeup of this committee is important, because it should be designed to be a policy-making body. Things like selecting new china, or purchasing silver trays, or what color napkins to use are important decisions but not for this committee. Their function is to support food service and serve as a buffer between it and the "shoulds." It probably is not necessary to have monthly meetings, but a yearly (quarterly?) review is recommended. Ask past chairs of the board or others who have held significant lay-leadership jobs to serve with the understanding that likely they will not be needed. But if they are, heavy hitters are wanted. Staffing the committee under these circumstances will not be hard, but remember that its members should be familiar with the food served. They eat at the church.

By the way, have you ever heard that a camel is a horse that was put together by a church committee?

Rule 6: Reservations are as important to food service as they are to Native Americans.

What Does My Crystal Ball Say?

Oh, ye predictor of events help me! The ladies of the church are planning an afternoon tea. "How many people are coming?" "We haven't the slightest idea." Well, goodness! It seems pretty obvious that if the planning group doesn't know, surely the food service director cannot be expected to know either. Often this conversation occurs in the church kitchen, and not just with ladies planning a tea. This seems not an appropriate position for either party.

The planners do not want to over-estimate their number so that they have to pay for no shows. The food service director does not want to hear that awful phrase, "They ran out of food!" because he was trying not to over-prepare. The horns on this dilemma are huge. Both parties have reasonable concerns, but let us share those concerns equally, and share the poor press, if there is any, equally also.

Sometimes for a first-time event, no one knows how successful it will be. Hopefully all involved can sit down together and reach an agreed-upon number, so that the kitchen does not take the publicity hit if more people come than anyone thought, or the financial hit if the number is substantially less. In order for food service to function efficiently and avoid red ink, it is necessary that it be given full information.

Meditation: A firm foundation is the wise and prudent use of facilities, and the expenditure of monies in appropriate ways. Stewardship is a whole lot more than money in the offering plate. It is about being circumspect before using up or wasting what has been given unto the Lord. Belshazzar was told he had been weighed on the scales and found wanting (Daniel 5:27), and so we are accountable to God for things with which we have been entrusted, be they monies, or volleyballs, or foodstuffs.

Chapter 7
Amazing Grace

I Corinthians 15:10 "But by the grace of God
I am what I am, and his grace to me was not without effect."

We learn from Abigail in I Samuel:25-44 that it is not necessary to have an impressive title in order to play a significant role. Abigail's husband, Nabal, was a wealthy man, having a thousand goats and three thousand sheep that he was in the process of shearing. It was therefore a festive time. David and his men had been protecting these animals and the shepherds night and day, and so when David asked Nabal to feed his 600 men, the request was part of the simple hospitality offered all travelers. It was not inappropriate to Nabal's assets.

Nabal answered that he saw no reason to take food he intended for his shearers and give it to men he did not know.

After all, they might be runaways, and he did not even know where they came from. When this was reported to David, he told his men to put on their swords, and he set out with 400 of them to seek vengeance on Nabal and his men for their insult and lack of appreciation for what David and his men had done for them.

Hearing of her husband's decision from a servant, Abigail quickly gathered 200 loaves of bread, two skins of wine, five dressed sheep, 5 seahs of roasted grain, one hundred cakes of raisins, and two hundred cakes of pressed figs and loaded them on donkeys. She set out at the head of this procession and literally cut David off at the pass. She said, "Let this gift be given to the men who follow you." David praised the Lord, and blessed Abigail for her good judgment. He told her that if she had not come to meet him not one male belonging to Nabal would have been alive at daybreak.

There certainly are "jerks" like Nabal everywhere, and the modern church has its share too. There is no guarantee that every member of every church will be Christ-like. There is no contract that says once you join the church all your bad habits and bad attitudes disappear. There are loyal church members who act in ways that are incomprehensible, some of them staff or even clergy. Having said all that wouldn't you rather deal with our jerks than with the jerks who have never committed to church membership and whose judgment is based solely upon what they think?

Those of us who eat frequently at a church, ours, or our neighbor's, or a family member's are blessed two ways: by the immediate fellowship we share with others, and by the rich heritage that has made it all possible. We have seen many stories here about those who got it all started, but the process is certainly not over.

There are new churches today and small churches today where the campus and membership are limited and always will be. There isn't much of a maintenance support system, and the good folk of the congregation put up and take down tables and then put chairs in place for a worship service that will occur shortly in the very same space. They do so without complaint and to the contrary, are energized because they know they are doing work for the Lord. The atmosphere in the rooms where they work is joyful, and they go about their task with a sense of fulfillment.

Not all food service happens at mega churches, and not all meals are prepared by employees. In fact it is likely that across America as many meals are prepared by volunteers as hired staff. They never heard of a jacketed kettle, but their food is wonderful, and they prepare it with the pleasure that comes from performing a real service. What follows is a tribute to all who serve as volunteers.

This brings to mind a word about the "work" done by volunteers in the kitchen. No church can function without the help of members of the congregation. They stuff envelopes, make posters, put flowers on the altar, help with funerals and weddings, and are part of endless planning and strategy sessions. They are an essential part of a successful church, and no church can operate without them.

Kitchen helpers, unlike the volunteers just mentioned, of course use their brain power, but it is their man-power that is most noticeable. They are on their feet constantly, carrying heavy items, going into the basement to get those items, lifting hot pots and pans, clearing used dishes, often washing those dishes, all done on hard-surface flooring. Their work is unquestionably more labor intensive. Coral Ridge Presbyterian in Florida has two volunteers who come in each week just to slice cases of tomatoes and wash lettuce for the salad bar. Volunteers in other churches make salads, or set tables, or arrange the child's food line, or get out condiments, or staff the food lines, or cook, or get needed items at the local grocery.

The food service volunteer is asked for more "elbow grease" than volunteers of other departments. The hours they work are not the usual hours either, nor is their work completed in a short time span. They come in late in the afternoon and stay well into the evening, or arrive at 6am to help with a breakfast. They see what method of service works best, what foods are favorites, who sits with whom. They are the first to notice changes in these habits. They are antennae to the congregation, and are unlike any other volunteer in any other program area.

Often volunteers are on the cutting edge in areas the church has not yet fully embraced. The "green" evolution of the 2000s is a burgeoning focus as we consider how our environment and our bodies are significantly affected by the food we produce and eat. All of the agricultural spectrum is under scrutiny about how our food is grown and harvested. In the 1940s and 1950s the food we ate was actually "organic" because modern methods of pest control and fertilization had not yet appeared in our farmlands. Today there is a great resurgence of interest in raising crops in the old way, but it is called "green" or "organic."

St. Bartholomew's Episcopal Church Atlanta, Georgia

Consider the volunteers of this church who have formed a "green team." Here is part of their mission statement:

"WHEREAS, we believe we bring harm to the earth through overproduction, unchecked consumption, and reluctance to employ alternatives thus creating disparity of energy and wealth among global communities and a dangerous environment for ourselves and future generations, we the green guild affirm our willingness and commitment to rebuilding a right relationship with God's earth."1

To this end, the St. Bart's volunteers have created a team of greenwashers who wash dishes for their Sunday breakfasts. Previously, these breakfasts were served on Styrofoam and plastic, and believing that these items damage the earth by never disintegrating, the team has replaced them with china each Sunday. The mission team of the church is beginning to serve coffee, organic, shade grown, and certified fair trade. They have obtained a large recycling bin, "binnie green," and are collecting paper to be remade into cardboard boxes which require 30-55% less energy to produce without sacrificing trees.

St. Bart's members also participate in a program called Community Supported Agriculture. By advancing a small amount of money to local farmers each family participating will receive a bag of produce weekly at the peak of ripeness.

All volunteer-led, this ministry is a significant part of the church's mission.

The Temple United Methodist Church
Russellville, Kentucky

This church celebrated its bicentennial in 2008; their goal was to honor the occasion by having 200 people at church each Sunday during the anniversary year. It was founded by a small group that met in individual homes to begin, and in 1808 it occupied its first building. In 1854 they moved to their present location, making a few changes and additions over the years. In 1917, after extensive remodeling including the installation of beautiful stained-glass windows, they occupied what is their present sanctuary. At that time they were called Russellville Methodist Church. When the remodeled church was first opened, a reporter came to write a story about it. He walked in, looked around, and remarked, "It looks like a temple!" The name stuck.

There has never been a paid food service person, but this doesn't mean there aren't skilled workers present in the kitchen....they just aren't given a salary for their labors. There are rotating teams assigned to the first week of the month, the second, and so on. If a meal is desired, a call is placed to Ruth Werth and she gets the appropriate team going. Ruth and her volunteers plan the menu, obtain the necessary supplies, and then prepare the Wednesday night supper for somewhere between 75 and 100 people. They also prepare meals for other events as well.

A great tradition of this church is their Tasters Lunch.

Held every year in October during the week-long Tobacco and Heritage Festival, this event features dishes prepared by the women of the church. It is advertised as taste tempting, and lives up to that reputation. Over 400 persons are served, and recipes from the lunch have been published in several cookbooks. Proceeds helped to purchase a new organ for the sanctuary and to make other significant improvements according to Evelyn Richardson, church historian.

First Methodist Church
Hutchinson, Kansas

In 1871 this soon-to-be church purchased the first lot sold in Hutchinson, and about 6 months later it was officially organized outside in a tent. They have occupied several buildings since then, the most recent one in 1972 when the sanctuary and fellowship hall were completed. They have a church history called *Saddlebags to Satellites* which accurately describes their growth and the changes they have seen since their inception.

The larger United Methodist Church has a program called Healthy Congregations in which First UMC participates. The Hallelujah Health Team serves healthy snacks between the services on Sunday and aims for members' spiritual, mental, physical, and social health.

Trinity United Methodist
Flagstaff, Arizona

This church began about 40 years ago in the auditorium of a local elementary school. In 1972 they occupied their first building which was a both a fellowship hall and a sanctuary, tables and chairs being replaced by rows of chairs for church services. There was a small kitchen with 1 home-style stove and refrigerator. The meals served at this time were all pot luck. By 1992, more space was needed, and in 2000 the church occupied a new family life center with its Celebration Hall—dontcha' love that name—which was a dining room when it was not being used as a basketball court. This means volunteers adding and taking off a cover on the floor to save it for the teams' use.

The volunteer food service operation is headed by Terry Schick and his wife. They prepare the Thursday (yep, Thursday) night supper two times each month, and a different set of volunteers works on the other two. The Schicks donate approximately twenty hours a week each on other church functions as well as these dinners, serving about 150 meals each week. Terry says there are perhaps 10 other volunteers working on food preparation and another two on clean-up. A big event for Trinity Heights is the annual women's retreat which involves three meals a day for over 100 women.

Trinity Heights is forward thinking. Their newest kitchen is equipped to serve 450 persons although no staff is yet in place to work there. They are preparing for the future, and hope to have a staff working sometime in 2009.

First United Methodist
Hudson, Florida

As near as they can tell Fellowship Dinners were started in 1999 by the church administrator and the senior minister's administrative assistant. They cooked the meals for about a month, and then due to a good response, they hired a cook from one of the local schools. Three others volunteered to help with the dinners, and they are still working to this day, serving about 100 persons each Wednesday.

In 2001 Doreen Engle and her husband retired and moved to Hudson. The church was $1,000. in debt with the dinners at this time. Doreen, who had worked as food service director at a large Atlanta church, volunteered to go over their menus and their ordering. Shortly thereafter, the one employee resigned, and Doreen offered to do the cooking and purchasing.

Several more volunteers came on board, and their all-volunteer food service was born. One of them is a gentleman who loves to cook and he and Doreen prepare most of the food. Six of them have attended classes and been certified by the local health department. Other volunteers are cashiers, or table decorators, or prep for peeling and cleaning 25 pounds of fresh shrimp, or workers on the clean-up crew including washing pots and pans. The volunteers are now so well-trained that they can be left in charge to manage a dinner on their own.

Several of Doreen's volunteers are widowers who felt

displaced when their wives died. Although still very welcome in the couples' Sunday school class, they no longer fit into the group. One by one Doreen recruited them to help in the kitchen, and these men now say they have once again found their place in the church.

One afternoon they went to the church to prepare a meal and were met by and "awful smell" which they knew right away was from spoiled meat. The refrigerator had broken. "Throw everything away, all of it!" Then they put a sign on the door that told diners there had been a problem and they should go out to dinner. This is one option the all-volunteer kitchen has that a staffed kitchen does not.

The $1000.deficit has become a $5,000 donation to the church, enabling the kitchen to purchase new commercial refrigerators and freezers. Their season is from October 1 to Mother's Day, and they serve up to 250 persons during the peak winter months. Professionally managed and professionally prepared by non-professionals, the meals at this church are delicious, served with style and smile.

Meditation: We have different ways of praising God, some do it with eloquent words; some do it with tambourine and flute; and some do it with pots and pans.

A Final Word

And it is indeed just that: a final word: Salt. Salt!

Nothing written about food and faith working together would be complete without mentioning salt. The earliest notable mention is, of course, when Lot's wife was turned into a pillar of salt because she disobeyed and turned around to see the destruction of Sodom and Gomorrah (Genesis 19:24). Transforming her in this way was entirely in keeping with the topography of the area where there were already bizarre salt formations. The act was not one intended to malign salt.

Leviticus 2:11 tells about the practice of sealing a covenant by eating a salt-seasoned meal. In this case it was the sacrificial meal, and the people were instructed not to omit salt from grain-offerings and sacrificial animals. Think about it, a readily-available item, not wine from a silver cup, or gold, but a common everyday thing available to everyone is the symbol chosen by God to seal a covenant....a food item.

Joshua 15 describes the boundaries of the tribe of Judah. In listing these boundaries, the salt sea is mentioned, as is Nibshan, called the city of salt.

2 Kings, chapter 3 describes the people of Elisha telling him that although the city had a good location, the water was bad. Elisha asked the people to bring him a new bowl with salt in it. He threw it into the pool of Jericho. In verse 23 we read, "Thus says the Lord, I have made this water wholesome never to cause death or miscarriage coming

from it." This was a miraculous fix once again using our very ordinary element.

The famous statement that "you are the salt of the earth" is mentioned in Matthew 5, Mark 9, and Luke 14. This statement registers. We know what is meant when we hear the words. All know the dimension and depth salt adds to food and bread. If salt loses its taste, it is worthless, and nothing will restore it to its usefulness. If we lose our connection to God, the same will be true of us. Important once again is the linking of this minor food item to a parable.

It started with the apple, and the journey continues today...Christian people eating and feasting together joyfully in God's house.

Bibliography

Albert E. Bailey: *Daily Life in Bible Times,* Charles Scribner's Sons, 1943.

Life Application Study Bible, New International Version, Tyndale House Publishers, 1997

William H. Gentz, General Editor, *The Dictionary of Bible and Religion,* Abingdon Press, 1986.

Ken Anderson, *Where To Find It In The Bible,* Thomas Nelson Publishers, 1996

NACFS Cookbook, 1992

Tony Campolo, *Who Switched The Price Tags?* Word Publishing, 1986

Allen J. Grieco, *The Meal,* Scala Publications, 1992.

A Moody Stuart, *The Three Marys,* The Banner of Truth Trust, 1984

Footnotes

1. Lois Coogle, *Tassels of Remembrance*, 1989. Page 3

2. Church Executive Magazine, May 2008, "The Pot Luck Supper Gives Way To Sophisticated Food Service Ministries," page 30

3. myersparkpres.org, History and Culture

4. Crossroads Community Ministries Special Report, undated

5. angelfoodministry.com

6. Wikipedia.com

With Special Appreciation to:

The Reverend Ron Greer, advisor and idea man.

The Reverend Charles Gardner who allowed me to use his library.

Teri Sawyer, former national president of NACFS, who as an author herself helped me know what will work and what won't.

And always to my dear friends and remarkable colleagues in the National Association of Church Food Service without whose experiences and input this book could not have happened.